IN THE WORDS OF GEOFF'S
PRIVATE CLIENTS

—— 99 ——

"Try and read this first before anybody else does."

— MANAGING DIRECTOR, INVESTMENT BANK

"A master craftsman, Geoff delivers a rare combination of personal experience and trenchant insight to help you supercharge your life. His passion is infectious. Blades has helped me develop critical tools to harness untapped personal reserves that have put me on a path to exceed stretch career goals."

— PARTNER, CONSULTING FIRM

"Success at the highest levels requires never-ending improvement. Geoff not only helps me to keep bringing my best, but to also feel more happy and energized every single day."

— PRESIDENT, BANK

"For two decades I have fervently studied success and worked with top coaches, but when I found myself overwhelmed with information and complexity, Geoff helped me cut through the noise and draw a straight and powerful path to getting what I want in my business and life...TODAY."

— FOUNDER, CEO, ACCOUNTING FIRM

"I came to Geoff when I was evaluating retirement. Geoff not only helped me quickly reach my decision to stay, he then helped me chart a course for taking my career to an entirely new level. Inside this book you will see some of the secrets that make him my secret weapon for success on Wall Street."

— Partner, Investment Bank

"After a decade of running my own firm and feeling like I was always a step behind, Geoff has me on track to building the business and life I truly love!"

— CEO, Public Relations Firm

"Working with Geoff has been transformational. He has changed the way I pursue specific professional goals, as well as how I think about my life overall. The time we have spent together has been invaluable."

— Partner, Investment Bank

"Geoff is a uniquely thoughtful and effective leader in the field of high achievement. You've been given the opportunity to read his exceptional book towards catalyzing breakout change both personally and professionally. Seize it. If you don't it will be your great loss. It's really that simple."

— Entrepreneur, Business Builder

"Right place right time. Some guys have all the luck. I used these excuses to rationalize my flattened career trajectory. Geoff helped me take calculated steps to break this cycle and reinvent myself, and thereby reattain happiness and fulfillment in my life."

— PRINCIPAL, INVESTMENT FUND

"I cannot say enough about Geoff. He gets to the heart of issues faster than anyone I have ever met. He is undoubtedly an important part of who I have become over these past few years...the best 'me' I have ever been."

— CFO, TECHNOLOGY COMPANY

"Geoff just gets it. He understands that our ability to achieve rests within our own abilities, and he allows you to unlock it. If you are committed to be your best, then you owe it to yourself to read this guide."

— MANAGING DIRECTOR, INVESTMENT BANK

"This is not just business for Geoff, it is intensely personal. For as long as I have known him this work has been his obsession, and Geoff has stopped at nothing to build mastery of these topics. Inside this guide you will see the ideas that have worked for him, me, and everyone he works with."

— FOUNDER, CEO, INVESTMENT MANAGEMENT FIRM

GEOFF BLADES

★ ★ ★ ★ ★

DO
WHAT YOU WANT

A CAREER GUIDE FOR
PROFESSIONALS SERIOUS
ABOUT WINNING

★ ★ ★

PUBLISHED BY:

LIONCREST
PUBLISHING

FOR PERMISSION REQUESTS, WRITE TO CONTACT@GEOFFBLADES.COM.

ISBN (Hardcover): 978-1-61961-403-1 | ISBN (Paperback): 978-1-61961-404-8

CONTENTS

PART 3: SCHEMING AND DREAMING

WHAT THIS GUIDE WILL DO FOR YOU

E very year the Gallup employee survey concludes that more than two-thirds of workers are either not engaged or actively dis-engaged in their jobs.

Growing up we're told that if we put our heads down and work hard that we can create the career and life of our dreams.

But how many of us are living our dream? How many of us are on track to make our careers and lives what we want them to be?

Not many. It seems even many people at the top are rarely satisfied with what they have achieved, and many are living lives of not-so-quiet desperation.

And we are the lucky ones! The majority of the world lives on less than ten dollars a day. So if we don't feel like we are winning, then who the hell does?

The truth is—putting your head down and working hard is not the answer. If you want to continue creating the career you truly want, you need a new system.

This guide is for transforming your career.

You might use this guide to make your career better, get paid more, get promoted faster, work fewer hours, or create more career options, but like using a Cray to multiple 2 x 2, you will miss the power of this guide.

This guide is for creating the boldest, most amazing career you can imagine. It is about figuring out what you truly love, creating your plan to get it, and building yourself into the person who can do it.

Each of us has some ideal in mind for the career and life we truly want. For some of us, this means powerfully driving our current career all the way to the top. For others, it means building a great career while also finding the right work-life balance. And still others dream of taking their career and life in a completely different direction.

The lucky ones have this all figured out. They're doing what they love and creating phenomenal success doing it. But many others are not so lucky.

When I began this work, I had no idea where it would lead me. I didn't even know where I *wanted* it to lead me, let alone how I would get there. I only knew that I wanted to find a better answer for my career.

It was a hard time on Wall Street, right after the Internet bubble burst, when I was based at ground zero—in Goldman's high technology investment banking group in Menlo Park. Before the bubble burst, I was a lifer and believed that as long as I put my head down and worked hard, my life would be everything I dreamed.

For a while, my put-your-head-down-and-grind-it-out philosophy worked well. It got me from my blue collar background to the top of my school and to landing the only job Goldman offered in Australia in my year. At Goldman, it got me promoted to associate after just two years. And it helped me land a plum transfer to the Menlo Park office in '99.

But after the Internet bubble burst, with half the office laid off, compensation slashed in half, and my career stalled in its tracks, I began to think differently.

Whereas in the past I happily accepted that Goldman was my life, I now began wondering what had become of my life.

Drawing up a pie chart of my life and looking at the small sliver labeled "not work," I wondered, *Is this the life I once dreamed of as a kid?*

I looked around at my colleagues, and I wondered, *How many of my friends are living their dream?* And looking years ahead to my bosses, I wondered, *Do I want their career? Do I want their life?* I didn't know.

So, with more questions than answers, one day I started a document entitled, "What Do I Want?" And I spent the bulk of the next decade reading thousands of books and writing thousands of pages of notes, figuring it out.

Taking control and putting these ideas to work, I transformed my career and life. Focusing clearly on what drives success I got more of what I wanted day to day, while at the same time I made a number of job changes that kept me moving toward my dream career and life.

Then, a decade after I began this work, I did what I never imagined I would do. I resigned from Wall Street to follow my obsession and teach people like you to do what you want.

In turning pro, despite having already spent tens of thousands of hours researching these ideas, I have gone far deeper. Investing multiples of the hours and the money I had invested in my university degree, I have trained with true masters of personal change and stopped at nothing to build mastery in personal development.

Nobody in the world does what I do. Bringing together top-tier business experience with the most advanced tools of human performance and expertise in personal change, I custom-build programs designed for getting my clients what they want in their business, career, and life.

While my client work is far-reaching, this guide is built to do only one thing—share with you my best ideas for doing what you want in your career.

Nothing like this guide has ever existed. Bringing together my best ideas for driving success in your career with the time-proven principles of success composed over the centuries by the world's greatest thinkers, this guide is a massive leap forward in personal and professional development.

But this guide takes it even further—much further—sharing with you a revolutionary system custom-built for doing what you want in your career.

This guide is intensely practical and built for getting results. I know these ideas work because they have been modeled after the most successful people I have researched, and they are the ideas I used to transform my own career.

More importantly, I know this approach works because for more than six years I have been putting these ideas to work, testing them in the most practical and demanding circumstances imaginable—in the careers of my senior private clients.

This guide offers no magic pill or "secret" to success but a powerful and straightforward approach to clearly defining what you want and then getting it. The approach you are about to learn can be stated in three simple steps:

1. DEFINE what you want (and you will learn how to do this even if you do not really know what you want).

2. DEVELOP and put to work a deliberate process for getting it.

3. BUILD yourself into the person who can do it.

This guide is not a touchy-feely book of rah-rah therapy. It is hard-core personal development. In doing what you want, even the best ideas are not enough, and you have in your hands the key to build you into the person who is big enough and bold enough to create the grandest vision you have for your career and life.

For more than fifteen years these ideas have been transforming my career and life, and I'm excited to share them here with you. You shouldn't have to read thousands of books to get what you want in your career, and this is the one book that I wish someone had handed me when I began this work. For doing what you want in your career, it is the only book you will ever need.

GEOFF BLADES
NEW YORK, NY

PART 1:
GETTING MOVING

CHAPTER ONE

THE TWO SECRETS FOR DOING WHAT YOU WANT

Do not go where the path may lead, go instead where there is no path and leave a trail.

— RALPH WALDO EMERSON

★　★　★　★　★　★

In 1994 Jeff Bezos was at a crossroad.

Having spent almost a decade building his career on Wall Street, he was well-positioned at the fast-growing and leading investment firm D.E. Shaw.

A pioneer in technology and investing, D.E. Shaw had already made a number of lucrative technology investments and Bezos was evaluating another, what he called "the everything store."

Bezos knew that if he pursued his vision for the everything store from inside D.E. Shaw he would never be a true owner, and if he wanted to achieve the financial rewards of an entrepreneur he would have to leave his job behind.

Newly married with a comfortable apartment on the Upper West Side of Manhattan, he contemplated his future.

Should he stay in a prominent and comfortable job or should he set out on his own to pursue his dream?

For Bezos, imagining looking back and regretting having not participated in the emerging Internet, it was a seemingly easy decision. He left his career and began building the everything store, Amazon.com.

All of us have a vision for what our career and life can be, yet for many of us the path isn't so clear. Do you stay in your current job? Make a move? Do something completely different? It's hard to know.

Many of us forever question what we want and our ability to create it, yet no matter who you are or what you want, we all want to know the same thing…

HOW DO YOU GET WHAT YOU WANT?

If you ask most people how to get what you want, they will start listing all the ways you can do more.

Step up, they'll say. *Add more value. Lean in. Work harder. Give* more. *Contribute more.*

Network more.

They might sound like decent ideas, but when will you find the time to do more?

You won't.

And you don't need to.

You are already networking. You are already contributing a lot, giving more, working harder, leaning in, and adding a lot of value.

You are already stepping the hell up.

You don't get more of what you want by doing more but by building a "directed career." This means that you are stepping back, clearly defining what you want, and developing a sophisticated approach for getting it.

Consider my client who came to me with the goal of making partner. Sick of putting his head down and working hard in hopes of getting promoted, he wanted to develop a winning strategy that would guarantee success. Stepping back from his career and clearly defining his specific strategy for winning, we built an approach that not only got him promoted, but required less work.

Thomas Edison said, "Being busy does not always mean real work. The object of all work is production or accomplishment and to either of these ends there must be forethought, system, planning, intelligence, and honest purpose, as well as perspiration."

That's what this guide is built to do.

NOBODY TEACHES YOU TO DO WHAT YOU WANT

As a child, you were never taught to do what you want. Rather, you were taught to do what your parents and teachers wanted! Your entire so-called education was laid out all the way through college. You were never required to figure it out. You were barely required to think. You were told what to learn, how to learn it, and you were given passing grades for regurgitating what others think.

But then, somewhat shockingly, it ends. Like a turtle hatching to scurry to the ocean, you graduate. You are on your own. Never having been taught how to get what you want, you are left to figure it out—somehow.

With pathetic guidance like, "Get a good job or follow your passions," it is little wonder that, as top psychologist Barry Schwartz writes in *Why We Work*, "Ninety percent of adults spend half their waking lives doing things they would rather not be doing at places they would rather not be."

If you go searching for answers in the shelves of personal development, you will likely get no closer to your answer. Most books presume you want what everyone wants—success, of course! Yet they offer no intelligent approach for figuring it out.

And while the guidance on *determining* what you want is terrible, most of the advice on *getting* what you want is downright painful. Success can feel nasty, brutish, and short because we are taught to put our heads down, grind it out, sacrifice, and give it all we have to get from A to B.

Even in school, where success is mostly contingent on reading and memorizing useless information, you are never taught basic skills like speed reading, nor are you taught memory techniques like the method of loci. Instead, you are taught that success is earned through hard work, sacrifice, and brute force.

The same is true in your career. Have you ever been taught the essential skills of success? Nope. Instead, you are shown your desk and expected to sink or swim. Many drown that way, others barely stay afloat, and even some of the most successful people are constantly worried whether they are swimming in the right direction.

LOOKING FOR A BETTER APPROACH

Parking in the back lot so no one would see me, I made a beeline into the Borders on Market Street—my *San Francisco Giants* cap pulled down over my face, dark glasses on, and Sony Minidisc in my ear.

Heading straight to the self-help section, I wondered: *What kind of people go over here?* I had seen enough Tony Robbins infomercials to think that none of this was for people like me. Yet, I was out of answers, so I went there with an open mind. I figured I would leave with one or two books.

That day, I left with thirty-three books and a new obsession for personal development, which since has led me to span both book ends. Going back in time, I devoured the old-school classics, learning centuries of wisdom from the world's greatest thinkers. And at the other end, I went New Age, opening my mind to Eastern philosophy and schools of esoteric knowledge, while covering all the business and other classics in between.

When I began learning these new approaches to success, it became obvious how limited my head-down, work-hard, step-up approach had been. It might have worked okay in a strong market that lifted all careers, but when the dot-com bubble burst, the many empty offices were proof that being the best workhorse in the office was not enough to build a great career.

By researching success and modeling the best, I came to see that the secrets to success are simple. But they are also hidden from plain sight.

THE TWO SECRETS FOR DOING WHAT YOU WANT

Read a bunch of books on personal development and you will see much the same thing. In the thousands of books, you will find millions of great ideas, but unfortunately almost all the books suffer the same fatal flaw. They are full of it: words, words, words, but little you can actually do with them.

The world doesn't need any more books on personal development, we just need better ones. Books filled with an endless collection of random ideas on motivation, planning, and thinking can be interesting, but you need little of that to get what you want.

When Steve Jobs challenged Apple to invent iPhone, he didn't take the best mobile phones and seek to make them incrementally better. He started from a clean slate of aluminum, asking, *How do you build the best mobile phone?*

Stephen Covey did the same thing. In writing one of the last truly innovative books on personal development, having examined centuries of research, he developed a revolutionary system that has come to serve millions of people.

This guide is built the same way.

Famously, Bruce Lee said: "Before I learned the art, a punch was just a punch, and a kick just a kick. After I learned that art, a punch was no longer a punch, a kick no longer a kick. Now that I understand the art, a punch is just a punch and a kick is just a kick."

In the beginning, the formula for success seemed simple—put your head down and work hard. Then, after a decade of research, success seemed incredibly complicated. I literally had thousands of pages of book summaries and thousands of pages of notes! But as I integrated the knowledge, through-lines began jumping out at me. Like looking at a scatter chart and trying to plot the straight line, once I understood the process deeply, the straight lines were all I could see. And I saw how incredibly simple doing what you want can be.

Like one kick and one punch, I boiled doing what you want down to two dominant ideas: *The Two Secrets for Doing What You Want.*

THE FIRST SECRET

In 1962, a man gave a speech that changed the course of humanity. During the height of the Cold War, and right before the Cuban Missile Crisis, he stood in front of a large crowd at Rice University and spoke of setting our sights on a goal far out of reach.

That man was then-President John F. Kennedy, and his words marked the beginning of the nation's conviction that it would indeed win the Space Race.

"The United States was not built by those who waited and rested and wished to look behind them. This country was conquered by those who moved forward—and so will space."

Another man who looked forward was a kid from a broken home born seven years earlier in California. A smart man, he seemed to be no genius but rather a directionless college dropout with great vision and the chops to think different. Like a shuttle blasting into space, Steve Jobs launched the Macintosh, hurling a sledgehammer at incumbent IBM before spending a lifetime disrupting and re-inventing, teaching us all to think different.

It seems that these two men had something in common that is lacking in ordinary humans, but the truth is that each of us has this same commonality buried inside.

What is that commonality? In a word: Conviction.

Definite Purpose.

The first secret for doing what you want is: You must know what you want beyond doubt, with such great conviction that you have definite purpose.

THE SECOND SECRET

The second secret for doing what you want is: You must have a process to get it.

You must reach beyond the random collection of millions of pages of books, blog posts, inspirational quotes, commencement speeches, tweets, and other next-best ideas to develop a far more sophisticated approach for getting what you want.

Consider, for instance, that after the financial crisis, much attention was directed toward the U.S. auto industry, whose collapse put hundreds of thousands of Americans out of work.

Naturally, people began asking: *What went wrong?*

The obvious culprit was Toyota's fuel-efficient Prius. Looking no deeper than the milk in their lattes, enamored by the innovation and technology, Mr. Everybody observed that Toyota was years ahead of the market, while American manufacturers were still producing gas-guzzlers.

But this was a simplistic understanding. To truly understand, one needed to look elsewhere; in time, that is—to after World War II, when the Japanese began applying a philosophy known as "Kaizen" to manufacturing.

Kaizen simply means "improvement" or "change for the best." Today, Kaizen is a process that is applied all over the world to healthcare, banking, human performance, and many industries outside of manufacturing. The driving concept of Kaizen is the simple idea that all things get better through a process of continuous improvement.

Kaizen = A Process of Continuous Improvement

This means that rather than haphazardly targeting your outcome, you instead develop a rigorous process for achieving your goal.

For doing what you want, you require more than good ideas, you require a system of continuous improvement. As Dilbert creator, Scott Adams wrote, "Losers have goals and winners have systems."

Laid out simply, The Two Secrets likely seem obvious to you. Yet in our society, when they should be plastered on every classroom wall, they remain hidden to everyone but the most successful people.

Consider President Obama. Whatever you think of him and his politics, surely you agree that his rise to the top was impressively maneuvered. He didn't just throw his hat in the ring and make it up as he went along. He spent years planning, seeing himself as President, learning the skills, and making moves positioning himself for the Oval Office. While his rise seems miraculous, it was driven by a powerful process.

As Formula One two-time world champion, Fernando Alonso, recently said: "Good things don't arrive by themselves; you need consistency and a method for everything you do in life."

The System for Doing What You Want! enables you to drive your career the same way.

THE SYSTEM FOR DOING WHAT YOU WANT!

This isn't just a system for doing any old thing. It is built specifically for one thing—doing what you want in your career. Remember, this approach is not for making your career a little bit better but for creating a powerful system that is built to make your career the best it can be. At any job and any level, you can take your career from where you are to wherever you want to be.

The System for Doing What You Want! works in five steps.

1. IN *DEFINE IT*, YOU LEARN an approach that solves the common problem of not knowing what you want. Let me repeat that: It solves the problem of not knowing what you want. So in just a few pages, your lifelong search for direction will be over! This powerful knowledge enables you to navigate the complexity and choice of your career. Beginning with the end in mind, you will develop your grandest vision for your career and your roadmap for getting there.

2. *GETTING IT* is the intelligence behind *The System*, where you clearly define how you get what you want. Here you step deep inside your career and ask yourself, what does it *really* take to win?

3.   IN *PLAN IT* you learn a simple, yet potent approach for creating your plan.

4.   IN *EXECUTE IT*, you will build an iterative, dynamic, and continuous process for executing your plan and getting what you want.

5.   FINALLY, *GETTING SKILLS* is where you will go far beyond the random books of arbitrary ideas for building skills and instead become focused on clearly defining what skills you need and apply a rigorous process for learning to quickly and powerfully build skills.

You will notice that The System comprises two separate components. The first four steps relate to the process of doing what you want, and the final step is the skills you require. I point this out because throughout this guide you will see these two powerful components—process and skills—coming together. Success requires both having a process for doing what you want and developing the skills to be able to do it.

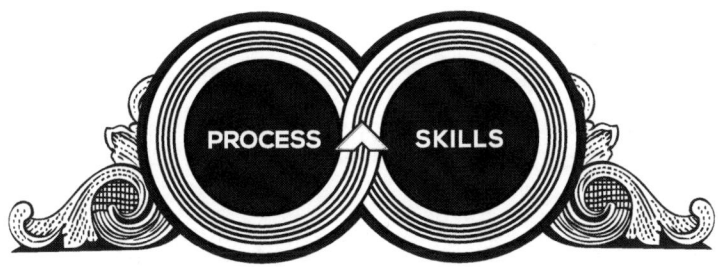

Putting it all together, *The System* is a fully integrated approach for doing what you want. Beginning with an advanced approach to figuring out what you want, it is built for taking you from where you are to wherever you want to be.

NOT A SEAT IN THE PARK

A confession: Many people who come across my work think it is too hard-core. And I'm the first to admit my approach is extreme.

That's because it is built for doing extreme things. It's not built for the average person to make his or her career a little bit better. It is for the select few who are looking to take huge leaps and make their careers and lives exactly what they want them to be.

When once asked about what leads to success, famous oil tycoon H. L. Hunt said, "First, decide exactly what it is you want. Most people never do that. Second, determine the price you're going to have to pay to get it, and then resolve to pay that price."

Most people don't have the balls for that. They simply do not want it enough.

To go after what you truly want, you must be a badass.

This guide is not for those with average ambitions, but those with their sights set on building an extraordinary career and getting remarkable results.

It is built for people like a client of mine who recently negotiated an eight-figure pay package. He didn't just walk into a meeting with his bosses. Stepping back from his career, he spent a number of months planning and strategizing the conversation. Then, by approaching his conversations with intent and using somewhat advanced tools of communications—yes-sets, pacing and leading, and language patterns—and framing his ask as a win-win outcome, his bosses didn't even try to negotiate with him.

Extraordinary results require an extraordinary approach.

This is how the most successful people on the planet approach success. Read *Grinding It Out* and you see the ways of thinking and systems Ray Kroc developed to build McDonalds. Or read *The Everything Store*, and you can see the vision and strategies that enabled Jeff Bezos to leave his career and build Amazon into a world-changing company.

A weekend runner might happily throw on a pair of sneakers and head out for a Sunday run, but a professional approaches their career differently.

While at first, the approach I have laid out for you might seem hard, the opposite is true. What most people are doing now is hard. It's a hard slog putting your head down and cranking away with no end in sight for the next forty years. Relative to how hard our careers can be, this guide is like playing a game of ping pong.

ONE CAREER TWO TRACKS

It's simple: You have to start from where you are. There's no other place to start. And there are only two different choices from here: You can move upward, or you can move out.

The trouble is: Many of us do not know what we want.

The approach you are about to learn takes this into consideration, showing you how to move forward in both tracks at the same time—driving forward in your current career track and exploring your other alternatives for creating the career you truly want.

Even if you do know that you want to leave your current career, you must leave from the right place. All your options will come from driving performance in your current career and building yourself into someone of great and unique value.

So the bulk of this guide is focused on powerfully driving value in your current career. Then we pick up in chapter 27: *Getting Out* and explore your alternative career tracks.

For those of you at more junior levels, I suspect you will find that the ideas in the earlier chapters are particularly helpful in getting established, and many of the topics will be of greater value as you progress in your career. That said, it is never too early to be approaching your career like a pro.

Those of you who are more senior might find some of the earlier ideas are helpful for framing your career, but it is the later chapters—such as *Getting It, Getting Paid and Promoted, Getting Out, and Beyond Your Career*—that you will find particularly valuable.

EXERCISE

In *Define It*, you will more specifically set goals, but as we are getting started it is helpful to consider what you are looking to get from putting this guide to work in your career.

Think about that for a moment. Ask yourself: *What am I looking to get out of my career? Am I looking for a solution to make it through the next two to three years? Am I focused on driving my long-term career track? Do I want to stay in my current role? Make moves? Do something completely different?*

And ask yourself what matters to you. Forget all the nonsense people spew about what should matter to you in your career, and ask yourself: *Am I focused on making money? Doing what I love? Do I want an exceptional career or am I happy with good enough? Do I really want to go for it, or am I just looking for a way to earn a good living? What else is driving me in my career?*

Really, be honest with yourself on what you want, and allow your motivators to cycle in your mind as you work your way through this guide.

CHAPTER TWO

TAKING ACTION

We've all been guilty at one point or another in our careers of boasting of perfect hindsight. It's a terrible sin. If you don't make sure your questions and concerns are acted upon, it doesn't count.

— JACK WELCH, WINNING

★ ★ ★ ★ ★ ★

Unless." This was the word that gave me the chills.

Let me explain.

I recently watched a TEDx talk by Larry Smith, a professor of economics who makes it his business to coach students to find a career they love.

The audience laughed when he dryly opened his TEDx talk with this line, "I want to discuss with you this afternoon why you will fail to have a great career."

He went on to cover the most common excuses people make for not taking the actions toward creating a great career. People will invent any excuse to fail or to take action, he said. They might even say things like this to their children ...

"I had a dream once, kid, but then you were born."

Have you ever said or thought something like that? *Everything changed when my kids were born and reality set in.* Or, *I had a dream, but then I got married, settled down, and I realized that dreams don't pay the bills.*

But Larry Smith asked it best: "Do you ever want to look at your spouse and your kid and see jailers?"

Rather than telling your loved ones that they will spend eternity having been locked up by some job that they hate, wouldn't you rather say, "Go for it, kid, just like I did!"

Larry Smith hits the nail on the head when he says:

"You won't be able to say that ... because you didn't.

"You are afraid to pursue your passion. Afraid to look ridiculous. Afraid to try. Afraid you may fail.

"Great friend. Great spouse. Great parent. Great career. Is that not a package? Is that not who you are? How can you be one without the other?

"But you are afraid. And that's why you are not going to have a great career.

"Unless..."

That's where I got the chills. He left us hanging.

And so that is where we now begin.

THE PROVISO

Your career can be what you want it to be, no matter what your career has been in the past. By defining what you want and developing *Your System,* you can create the career you truly want.

Like if you decided you were going to challenge yourself and run a marathon, by developing the right approach and working at it consistently over time, you can achieve any goal you set your mind to.

It's that simple. But there's a proviso—a big proviso.

You must be willing to do what it takes to make it happen. Creating the career you truly want does not just happen automatically because you pick up this guide. It happens when you put to work these ideas and take action.

As Napoleon Hill wrote, "Millions of people falsely believe that knowledge is power. It is nothing of the sort! Knowledge is only potential power. It becomes power only when, and if, it is organized into definite plans of action and directed to a definite end."

Doing what you want is a force of will. It requires taking the necessary actions for as long as needed so that you get what you want.

Of course to have made it this far in life you are already the type of person who takes action and makes things happen, but creating the career you truly want requires more than the same type of action.

While taking the actions that have worked well for you in the past is important, for most people this is simply not enough.

Instead, in doing what you want, you must be willing to take certain types of actions:

1) YOU MUST BUILD WINNING HABITS.

2) YOU MUST BE WILLING TO DO HARD THINGS.

3) YOU MUST TAKE CONTROL AND DRIVE CHANGE.

4) YOU MUST GRAB HOLD OF YOUR CAREER AND GO AFTER IT!

5) YOU MUST FOCUS ON DEVELOPMENT.

6) YOU MUST AIM FOR MASTERY.

7) YOU MUST TAKE RISK.

1

BUILD WINNING HABITS

Read biographies of leaders and you will learn many secrets of success. Read enough of them, and you will notice obvious patterns emerging. Although you will see many individual secrets, you will observe they are tied together by one common theme:

Winners know what leads to success, and they are exceptional at building the habits of winning.

Research someone successful who you admire, and you will see the same thing. Whether it be Michael Jordan, Elon Musk, Abraham Lincoln, or anyone else, you will see that it wasn't their gifts and talents that led to their success, but the cultivation of powerful habits.

As Vince Lombardi put it, "Winning is not a sometime thing; it's an all the time thing. You don't win once in a while, you don't do things right once in a while, you do them right all the time. Winning is a habit. Unfortunately, so is losing."

In *The Power of Habit*, Charles Duhigg writes, "Duke University research-ers in 2006 found that more than 40 percent of the actions people performed each day weren't actual decisions, but habits," and winners cultivate winning habits.

The difference between mediocre and extraordinary careers is much smaller than most people think. Evolutionary improvement leads to revolutionary outcomes, and the secret is building habits of continuous improvement.

This is the theme you will see throughout this guide. You are not just hap-hazardly taking actions, trying to eek out a win or two here and there. Instead, you are developing your habits of winning, which lead you to re-peatedly take the right types of actions.

2

DO HARD THINGS

Founder and former CEO of Southwest Airlines, Herb Kelleher, said, "In my spare time I work, seven days a week, usually until 8 or 9 o'clock at night."

As Malcolm Gladwell wrote in *Outliers*, "The people at the very top don't work just harder or even much harder than everyone else. They work much, much harder."

This guide asks you to do something even harder: Do hard things.

Look at the world around you. People who work harder aren't necessarily successful. Truly successful people do hard things.

Any fool can keep working harder and then much, much harder. Sure, putting your head down, cranking away, and hoping you get what you want feels hard. It is hard.

But relative to doing hard things, it's easy to work harder.

In his book, *The Hard Thing About Hard Things*, leading founder and venture capitalist, Ben Horowitz writes, "That's the hard thing about hard things—there is no formula for dealing with them."

Doing hard things requires taking actions that are uncomfortable: doing new things, growing, learning, and being terrified but taking actions anyway. It requires setting goals that you are uncertain you can achieve. Exposed to failure, you put yourself on the line. That's hard for most people.

But what's harder? Staying in your comfort zone and living a shadow life, or doing hard things and going for what you truly want?

3

DRIVE CHANGE

The first habit of highly effective people, according to Stephen Covey's ground-breaking book is: Be proactive. In this guide, being proactive means taking control and driving change.

If you are not in control of your career, then your career is out of control. The truth is that little of your career is within your control, which makes it all the more important to control what you can.

Taking control means ensuring you are positioned correctly. Every job in every company connotes a different type of career track, and it is up to you to ensure you are positioned in the right job and in the right way to win. Know how your business wins, and most importantly, position yourself to win. Taking control of your career means driving change.

Mark Zuckerberg's hacker motto is: "Move fast and break things." The idea, he explains, "is that if you never break anything, you're probably not moving fast enough."

Leaders are not only great problem solvers, they are problem creators. Leaders know problems contain the seeds to their solution, so in creating and solving problems, they are driving continuous improvement.

So if your career ain't fixed, break it! Rather than waiting for a problem to strike—for instance, being managed out—take actions to keep disrupting your career and forcefully moving toward what you want.

4

GO AFTER IT!

In her book, *Lean In*, Facebook COO Sheryl Sandberg writes, "We hold ourselves back in ways big and small. By lacking self-confidence, by not raising our hands, and by pulling back when we should be leaning in."

The same is true in getting what you want: To win, rather than hanging back, go after it! Put your best foot forward.

Think of it this way—two types of fighters compete in boxing. Counter-punchers, like Floyd Mayweather, Jr., wait for their opponents to come to them. Swarmers, like Mike Tyson, bring the fight to you.

In your career, you must be a swarmer. There's no counter-punching strategy. In getting what you want, you must lean in.

But note, leaning in is simply not enough, and getting what you want requires understanding your firm's rules of success and playing the game.

It's like playing chess. Before you are ready to learn strategies to win and make your opening moves, you must first understand the rules of the board.

That requires learning the rules of engagement in your firm. Nobody will teach you these rules. They are not written down anywhere. It's up to you to develop a sophisticated understanding of the players and the rules, and play them to win.

5

DEVELOP

In 1894, Orison Swett Marden wrote: "While many are surprised in their lack of success, few appear to attribute this to the fact that they are doing little to pursue growth."

One of the problems for many people is that their skills have become commoditized. Whereas in the old days, you could reasonably expect to keep progressing so long as you were doing a good job, today's game has changed.

As my client put it, "When my kid was interviewing to get into pre-school, like copping a steel pipe to the head, it was clear I needed to raise the bar." To compete at a higher level, you must have higher capabilities.

In *The Magic of Thinking Big*, former chairman of General Electric Ralph Cordiner is quoted as saying, "We need from every man who aspires to leadership—for himself and his company—a determination to undertake a personal program of self-development. Nobody is going to order a man to develop ... Whether a man lags behind or moves ahead in his specialty is a matter of his own personal application."

The future of learning is personal development, and those who develop will lead. Leaders are readers. And leaders are consistently focused on driving success through developing expertise.

Any athlete knows that getting different results requires changing it up and hitting it differently. Many professionals resist: They keep doing more of the same hoping for different results, but champions think differently.

Up until a few years ago, Andy Murray was a top-two-ranked tennis player with three grand slam finals, but failing to win a crown. Then, with the spirit of a champion, he made a dramatic change that transformed his game.

Ahead of the 2012 season, Murray visited Ivan Lendl and asked him to coach him in his unique approach to playing the game.

That decision transformed Murray's game and his career, leading him to win the U.S. Open, Olympic Gold, and the elusive Wimbledon crown.

6

TARGET MASTERY

Ray Dalio runs the largest hedge fund in the world for many reasons. He writes about one of them in *Principles*: "I often hear people say, 'It's getting better,' as though that is good enough, when 'it' is both below that bar and improving at an inadequate rate. That isn't good enough."

Consider my client Dean. When Dean walks into a meeting, he knows why he is there. He knows his ask, and he has designed the meeting to get to the ask. He knows who he needs to be, how to position himself and his firm, and he has profiled the client. Dean knows what drives him, how he thinks, and what he values. He even knows when he is creating pictures in his mind while he speaks. He acts strategically with intent, bringing the most advanced tools and skills. He is exceptional at reading people, controlling conversational frames, and using persuasive language and narrative to drive emotion in every meeting.

None of this has happened by accident. He has learned this because he is dedicated to achieving mastery.

Mastery comes from exceptional dedication to excellence. Kanye West said it took him five thousand hours to create one song, "Power." Even if he were working around the clock, that is more than six months, for one song that runs four minutes and fifty-two seconds!

Mastery doesn't come easily. As Albert Einstein said, "Only one who devotes himself to a cause with his whole strength and soul can be a true master. For this reason, mastery demands all of a person."

For a professional footballer, mastery does not happen by picking up the ball and running with it. And no one imagines that thousands of hours of welding on a production line qualifies you to be CEO of Ford. The key to an exceptional career is building mastery at the right things.

It is easy to see how targeting mastery and driving *Your System* through continuous improvement builds you into someone of great and unique value, which is an unstoppable formula for doing what you want.

—— 7 ——

TAKE RISK

A colleague left Goldman Sachs as a vice president to start his own boutique investment bank, though he had just one client and one deal.

Launching his own firm was just the beginning. A tenacious and relentlessly hard-working guy, he ferociously went after it: building relationships, chasing down deals, executing on more and larger transactions.

He quickly built a powerful brand and dominant franchise. And, he made a fortune.

There are many reasons for his out-sized success, but they all come back to one: He took risk, and he kept taking it.

Netscape co-founder Marc Andreessen recently said, "The issue is that without taking risk, you can't exploit any opportunities... You can live a quiet and reasonably happy life, but you are unlikely to create something new, and you are unlikely to make your mark on the world."

In a discussion at Stanford Business School, billionaire investor, George Roberts, discussed how he, his cousin, and former colleague left their jobs and started their own firm. The title of the video tells the story: "Don't Miss Opportunities."

And that's the real nut. Every day people miss opportunities because they are unwilling to take risks.

Many people trick themselves into avoiding risk by saying they are "risk averse." What matters is not whether you label yourself risk averse, but rather what your definition of risk is.

There is little risk, for instance, in sitting quietly in a meeting, but you are also failing to add value. You risk speaking up and having your ideas shot down, yet adding value is your greatest source of opportunity.

So which one is *really* more risky?

GET MOVING!

All the ideas for taking action are for naught unless you are actually taking action. And taking action is for naught unless you are committed to keep taking action all the way until you get what you want.

In Hollywood, we often hear of the many years it takes to become an overnight success. As Monty Hall famously said, "Actually, I'm an overnight success, but it took twenty years."

And although *The System* you are learning is designed to work fast, every aspect of this approach orients you to think long-term.

Rather than encouraging you to wake up one day and make some catastrophic career change, you are learning a methodical approach to taking deliberate action over time.

Not only does this make change feel methodical and easy, but it also removes the number-one constraint many face in making change: Big change waits … and waits … and waits.

The Chinese have a proverb that the best time to plant a tree was twenty years ago. The second best time is now. Sure, it would have been nice to have started this approach years ago, but the steps you take now will build the vision for your career. The question is: Will you get started?

What is interesting about taking action is that it can be incredibly hard to get started, but there is no stopping a rolling ball. The first step is almost always the hardest.

I recently received an email from a friend I have been casually guiding for a few years. One of the brightest people I know, like most who pretend they want to make a change, he had failed to take any meaningful step. But a few months ago, he had a breakthrough. He wrote me, "Making this change is very, very daunting, which is why I think I have not done this already."

Your first few small steps. They can be simple and small, but you must take them. Rather than waiting for the perfect time to take the perfect action, start today, and take any action that gets you moving.

What matters more than whether your first step is a baby step or a giant leap is whether you have the conviction to establish a consistent habit of taking steps over time.

As Jenny Craig said, "It's not what you do once in a while; it's what you do day in and day out that makes the difference."

I meet with my clients one hour a week, and that's all you need. If you are doing this right, you put this guide to work every hour of your career and get more of what you want in less time.

Simply a small weekly commitment can make your career unrecognizable in a couple of months, let alone after a year. Are you committed?

CHAPTER THREE

STARTING WITH YOU

Nothing can stop the man with the right mental attitude from achieving his goal; nothing on earth can help the man with the wrong mental attitude.

— THOMAS JEFFERSON

★　★　★　★　★　★

You commonly hear the phrase, "You are what you eat," but that is inaccurate. You are what you think.

Your thoughts drive everything you do—and I mean *every-thing*—and there is nothing more important to doing what you want than how you think. In taking actions and putting *The System* to work, your thinking is everything, which is why before we get to *The System*, we are starting with you.

While you can find many good books on thinking and mindset, most are extremely limited in comparison to what I train my clients to do.

DO WHAT YOU WANT

If you want to create the career you truly want, you must first start by building yourself into the person who can do it.

You see, there are two parts to getting what you want.

The first part, the most obvious part that you will find in every book on personal development, focuses on the tasks you must do: set goals, develop your plan, and execute. This is an important part of this guide, but it is only one part of getting what you want. On its own, a task-focused approach is severely limiting because it implies success is all about taking steps.

But more important than the steps you take is finding the answer to this question: *Who is the "you" who will take the steps?*

Rather than seeing success as simply "you" taking steps, instead ask who you must become for doing what *you* want.

I know that might sound airy-fairy, so let me give you a rock-hard example.

Consider an Olympic weightlifter who has his sights on lifting a world record. Looking at this vision one way, his goal appears task-focused: He succeeds by lifting a bar stacked with weight. But that is the outcome he is targeting, and he achieves success first by building himself into a bigger, stronger, person capable of lifting a world record weight.

This is worth repeating: The steps he takes to achieve his goal relate not to the task, but to building himself into the person who can succeed.

Consider if you ask one hundred campaign experts how Barack Obama became president. They could discuss *ad nauseam* all the things he did successfully during his campaign: raising $1 billion, developing a popular message, courting media, and so on. And although they would surely come up with a long list, I suggest that the list is secondary to what he did first:

He built himself into the man capable of becoming president.

Imagine you are looking ahead in your career thinking about how you get promoted. You would certainly begin to write a list of what you must do, but first and foremost you want to ask: *Who must I become?*

WHAT PERSONAL DEVELOPMENT SHOULD BE

Whereas many people (including many so-called experts) think of personal development as setting goals, developing plans, positive thinking, and so on, a you-focused approach is the crux of personal development.

This is how top athletes develop their potential. They imagine themselves standing in the center of the podium with gold slung around their necks. They do not just focus on what they must do, but moreover on developing the capabilities for making it possible.

Top performers know that personal development is about getting more of what you want by increasing your capabilities in three ways.

1.   THE FIRST WAY is by increasing your task-focused capabilities and doing the right things to have more impact in everything you do. Just by this, even if you are the same old regular you, you will massively increase your capabilities for getting what you want. This is what we are doing throughout this guide.

2.   THE SECOND WAY you increase your capabilities is by developing skills, which you are already doing, but more specifically we cover in the final step of *The System* called *Getting Skills*.

3.   THE THIRD WAY you increase your capabilities is by training your mind and learning to think different!

FOLLOW YOUR HEART, BLAH, BLAH, BLAH

During one of my presentations at Stanford Business School, I showed one of the most popular quotes from Steve Jobs' famous 2005 Stanford commencement speech on the screen:

Your time is limited, so don't waste it living someone else's life. Don't be trapped by dogma—which is living with the results of other people's thinking. Don't let the noise of others' opinions drown out your own inner voice. And most important, have the courage to follow your heart and intuition.

Then I asked three questions:

1.   "How many of you love that quote?"

I was met with nods and smiles from all across the room.

2.   "How many of you know what it means to you?"

I lost some of the room but many kept nodding and smiling.

3.   "How many of you have the courage to follow your heart?"

With this, nods turned to stillness. Smiles turned to blank stares. In three questions, dreamers turned to stone.

Sitting in your comfortable seat, it is easy to dream of the possibilities for your career and imagine feeling what it is like to follow your deepest desires. Like soaking up the sunshine, relaxing with your feet dipped in the sand at your favorite beach, you can sink into that feeling.

But then something begins to change.

Your imagination shifts from dreaming into what it takes to *do* it. Your mind starts racing: *What must I do? How will I do it? Is it possible?*

Weighing the gravity of the change, instead of dipping your feet into sand, perhaps now it seems you are standing on the edge of a cliff. Thinking about jumping, your excitement is replaced with fear. You are no longer soaring, but looking down into the nothingness in which you might descend.

That feels hard—painstakingly hard. Whereas before you were excited about taking actions, now you are on edge and there is no way you will jump.

Your actions have changed along with your thinking. This simple cognitive-behavioral model from psychology shows you why.

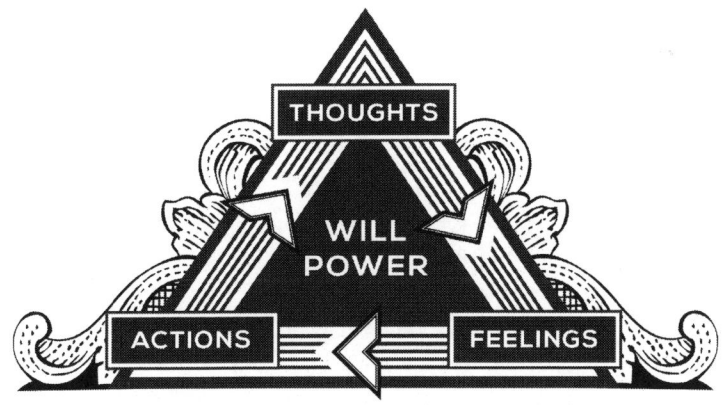

This is how your mind works. Your thoughts drive your feelings and your feelings drive your actions. In a cycle, round and round you go. In our example, when you are dreaming, you feel inspired to take actions. Yet, when you change your thinking and imagine yourself standing on a cliff about to jump, you change your feelings, and so too your actions.

And that is why it does not matter how many inspirational quotes you read or how many times you watch Steve Jobs' commencement speech or the TEDx presentation by Larry Smith or every motivational speaker on the planet. No matter how much you fill your mind with ideas, you will fail to take action, unless...

You choose the thoughts that are driving your feelings and actions.

And this is why "willpower" is at the center of this model.

Doing what you want requires consciously choosing your thinking, training, and conditioning your mind for taking actions.

★   ★   ★   ★   ★   ★

THINK AND DO WHAT YOU WANT

In his book *Tribes*, paraphrasing the Peter Principle, Seth Godin writes, "I think what actually happens is that in every organization everyone rises to the level at which they become paralyzed with fear."

No matter what you want and no matter what it takes to get it, doing what you want begins with choosing your thinking.

To have the freedom to dream and set your sights on what you truly want, you must think it is possible. To create your plan and take the execution steps, you must think they will get you what you want. In this and every other way, your thinking drives your actions in doing what you want.

Imagine you are sitting around thinking you have zero chance of getting promoted to the job you want and also have limited options to leave.

Allowing yourself to choose "low-value thoughts" and thinking you are stuck with limited options, you would likely feel unmotivated, which is unlikely to drive you to take steps to get promoted. You will fail to get promoted, which will reinforce the thinking that you are going nowhere, which in turn will reinforce your "downward spiral" into more negative thinking, feelings, and actions.

This is common thinking.

If, however, you choose "highest-value thoughts," you will create different feelings and actions. Even if you believe your chances are limited but within the realm of possibility, highest-value thoughts will allow you to choose to give it your best shot. That gets you feeling energized, which leads you to take constructive actions.

Hence, you are more likely to get promoted. Even if you fail you maintain an "upward spiral," choosing the thinking that keeps you moving in the right direction. Here you not only choose the thoughts that feel good, but you also increase your chances of getting promoted in the future and create other options.

This example shows the way your thinking "spirals," either positively or negatively. Your thoughts trigger feelings, which trigger actions—and round and round again—ultimately changing and defining what is possible for you.

★ ★ ★ ★ ★ ★

YOU CHOOSE YOUR THOUGHTS

In choosing your thoughts, it is important to recognize the difference between "reality" and your perception of reality.

To the uninitiated, thinking happens to them.

They get cut off on the street and immediately respond with the finger. They shout, "That makes me so mad." Yet, as you become familiar with these topics, you recognize that only you can choose your thoughts.

In the same way that you can choose to pick up your phone when it rings, you can always choose how you respond to external stimuli.

This means that choosing how you think is always within your power, no matter what is going on around you, no matter what is happening in your life, and no matter what is the so-called "reality" of your career. At an extreme, you can always feel how you want, irrespective of your conditions.

While that might sound all good in theory, of course it can be extremely hard in practice. That is because you are choosing many of your thoughts unconsciously, as a matter of habit and repetition.

Your patterns of thinking are mostly established in your mental blueprint by age six, and from then on, they are mostly repeated.

Consider trying to convince an atheist to accept God, or a die-hard Republican to vote Democrat. Although they might consider themselves open-minded, you will probably never make a dent.

Your mind does not start from a blank slate when it thinks. It is efficiently referencing your past memories, decisions, experiences, values, and beliefs.

So, while you might think you are open-minded and willing to evaluate new ideas, often you are simply running new ideas through old thought patterns, remembering what you already think.

Furthermore, about ninety percent of your thinking is redundant, which means that almost everything you are thinking today is the same thing you were thinking yesterday, and it is the same thing you will think tomorrow.

This is why I say that you are hardly choosing your thoughts, so much as they have been "chosen" for you by habit and repetition.

Fortunately, you can easily train new habits of thinking.

CHOOSE THE THOUGHTS THAT
SERVE YOU

A cat catches a glimpse of itself in a mirror. Noticing the "other cat," it attacks the mirror or quickly scurries away. A woman looks at a photo of herself and automatically recognizes that face on a two dimensional print, noting, "That's me."

While a leopard can't change its spots, human beings were born with something that definitively sets them apart from all other creatures: We have reason and willpower. So while a cat has no cognitive ability to even know it is a cat, you as a human have the ability to think critically—to use your mind and choose your thoughts.

Just as you have the ability to recognize your picture, you have the ability to recognize patterns of thinking. And once they are recognized, you have a choice to either keep reinforcing old patterns or build new patterns of thinking.

You do that in two steps: first by choosing the thoughts that serve you in getting what you want, and second, by practicing your new thinking and training new habits.

★　　★　　★　　★　　★　　★

BECOMING LIMITLESS!

What if I offered you a pill that would unlock your capabilities and allow you to use one hundred percent of your brain?

Would you take it?

I would. And quite frankly, I have tested plenty of smart and not-so-smart drugs looking for it.

Yet I kept coming back to one powerful conclusion—you already have a limitless mind! You just need a way to train it.

In all my years researching personal development, and in training with some of the best teachers in the world, I discovered many great ideas and tools for training your mind. Yet, I failed to come across any system for putting them to work.

So going one step beyond aggregating the best ideas and tools, I developed a powerful system for training my own mind. My *System of Your Limitless Mind* has three steps.

1. THE FIRST STEP relates to choosing your thinking. Here, you are determining the thoughts you want to think.

2. YOU USE THE PERFORMANCE TOOLS for mental training. Like hitting the gym, these are the equivalent of exercises.

3. FINALLY, like the program you use for getting in shape at the gym, you want a process for choosing your thinking and applying the tools.

The first draft of this guide was three times this length and included more than one hundred pages on training your mind. You see, mental training and conditioning are so important to doing what you want that this section was originally long enough to create a separate book. I decided to condense this section and go ahead and create that second book because of the gravity of this idea. Your thinking is essential to doing what you want. I cannot underscore this point enough. The importance of thinking to doing what you want is so great that I spend at least half my time with clients training their thinking.

Because your thinking is driving everything you do, there is nothing more important to doing what you want than training your thinking. So I strongly suggest you not only read the next section carefully (and come back to it over and over again) but you also do more than read by taking the ideas and practicing the tools.

CHAPTER FOUR

TRAINING YOUR LIMITLESS MIND

The greatest discovery of my generation is
that a human being can alter his life by altering his
attitudes of mind.

— WILLIAM JAMES

★　　★　　★　　★　　★　　★

Earlier we discussed how your thinking drives your feelings, which drive your actions. We also said that as long as you are choosing your thinking, why not choose your highest-value thoughts that get you taking the actions for getting what you want?

Some people might describe this as positive thinking. I just call it THINKING! You are in control of your thinking, and you choose the thinking that benefits you. That's not positive thinking—it's just thinking!

And, why would you possibly consider thinking in any other way?

Now, the cynical types might say, *Well, it's not realistic.*

They miss the point. It's neither realistic or unrealistic. There are no judgment calls with thinking. You simply choose to think in a way that gets you feeling like taking the actions that make things possible.

What I'm about to share with you is far beyond some generic list of ideas on mindset. Rather it consists of specific ways of thinking for putting *The System* to work. These ideas are designed to help you do three things:

1. GIVE YOU the freedom to dream, to get beyond the boundaries of "realistic" thinking and open your mind to limitless possibilities.

2. GET YOU taking actions.

3. GIVE YOU TOOLS that inspire persistence, so you will keep taking actions all the way to getting what you want.

BOUND BY LIMITED THINKING?

As kids, we all dream freely, imagining that anything is possible. But then, over time and through social conditioning, like Captain Trips spreading from person to person, "realistic" thinking settles in, killing most dreams and dreamers. You will remain the walking dead unless you change it.

While it might not seem easy to remove your limited thinking, it is actually just a matter of changing a number of small thoughts.

It's like the story in *Gulliver's Travels* where Gulliver finds himself as a giant on the island of Lilliput, which is inhabited by tiny people. Upon awakening, Gulliver discovers that the tiny people have tied him to the ground with many tiny strings. Although he could easily break any one of the strings, he remains trapped by the great number of tiny strings binding him.

The same is true with your thinking. Although it might seem you have been limited by powerful thoughts, you will see upon close examination that they are merely an aggregation of puny thoughts. And by choosing bigger, better thoughts, you can easily break free.

FOCUS ON LIMITLESS THINKING

Many people's minds are swimming in the mental sewers, constantly engrossed in limited thinking such as pessimism, depression, anxiety, insecurity, worry, fear, cynicism, and so on.

While in some cases it is appropriate to medicate these "diseases," at least temporarily, this often keeps people stuck in limited thinking.

What even many medical professionals fail to consider is that where attention goes, energy flows.

You don't shovel the darkness out of a room. Instead you flick a switch and let light flood the room, and good personal change works the same way.

So rather than putting your attention and energy into the thinking you want to stop, instead flip it the other way and put all your attention and energy into the thinking you want to grow.

For instance, rather than trying to stop being cynical and pessimistic, instead ask yourself: *What is a future scenario that gets me excited and optimistic?* Similarly, rather than focusing on what makes you anxious, instead imagine your future playing out even better than you expected. Then get focused on taking the actions to make it so.

Similarly, and this is a big one, rather than being bound by your fears, such as the debilitating fear of failure, instead ask yourself: *What actions would I be taking if those fears were behind me?*

Then, take the actions and put those fears behind you!

Look, I recognize it might not always be as simple as this, but do it. Learn to command your mind because in many cases, it really *is* this simple.

Taking this notion to the extreme is a concept I call "building you." This means that rather than focusing on what you want to change, orient all of your thinking to what you want to feel, do, be, and have.

BUILDING YOU

A man stands naked in front of the mirror and says to himself, "I've gotten fat. I really should exercise more."

He has already shot himself in the foot. In using the word "should," he has turned weight-loss into something that is not what he "wants" to do.

Then he says to himself, "Man, if only I looked as good as I used to look." Now, he is limited by who he was in the past and regretting that he is not what he used to be.

After work, when he "should" go to gym, he finds himself thinking that he does not really feel like going. He wonders why.

Think back to the cognitive-behavioral model, and you will remember that it is because of the thoughts he is feeding into his body. He is imagining how it requires all this effort and how hard it feels.

The result is that he either skips out and keeps his old habit, or he goes, but with the wrong motivation and focus, he has a half-assed workout, in which case he will fail to see results over time and ultimately stop going.

Building you is the act of choosing your thinking so that you have the right frame of mind to put the tools and process to work.

Think of a time in your life when you lacked confidence. Perhaps you still do. Maybe you feel really insecure about making presentations. In the past, you might have come to accept this lack of esteem as "who you are." Unable to easily change it, you find yourself worried about how this lack of confidence has been holding you back.

Rather than being held back, why not learn to flip your thinking?

Rather than thinking about the problem of lacking confidence—or lying on a couch digging into your past and trying to "understand" how you got that way—instead focus on: *How will I be presenting with more confidence?*

Rather than focusing on that person who lacks confidence, you begin to see that person—you!—as confident.

From these images of yourself as confident, you begin adding teeth to your thoughts. Bringing all the force of your imagination into play, you wonder: *Who am I when I am more confident? How do I walk? Talk? Am I more assertive? Appear stronger? What else am I now capable of doing?*

Once you design this new person in your mind, you can build yourself into that person using the tools and processes we will now cover.

THE THINKING AND THE TOOLS

Coming up, I will share ten types of limitless thinking and ten performance tools you can use to train your thinking.

It bears noting that some types of mental training might be unnecessary. You might be able to change them simply by saying: "Yep, I've chosen to be confident."

It's not that easy in other cases, which is where the tools and the process can help you condition new ways of thinking.

For instance, you might get tremendous value from reading powerful quotes, such as Aristotle's: "We are what we repeatedly do. Excellence, then, is not an act, but a habit." But in order to fully integrate this idea, you want simple tools you can put to work each day in building powerful habits.

Another reason you want the tools and process is because of the type of mental training we are doing here. See, there are two types of personal change.

The first type, known as remedial change, is about fixing problems, such as overcoming a fear or changing a habit. While with the right tools wielded by the right person, remedial change can be decidedly easy, that is not what we are doing here.

We are doing something much harder, which is the second type of personal change: generative change. We are not looking for a one-time solution.

Instead, we are building a system to train your thinking all the way to building you into whomever you choose to be.

Think of the difference between remedial change and generative change akin to the difference between someone hitting the gym for a few weeks to lose a few pounds and someone looking to get in shape for an Ironman and then get better, faster, and stronger year after year. While the first person needs a one-time solution, the latter requires a system that challenges him on an entirely different level.

So remember, reading these ideas is not enough. You want to keep coming back to these ideas over and over again, conditioning your thinking and building the mental muscles of your limitless mind.

—— **1** ——

TAP INTO YOUR BURNING DESIRE

The truth is, most people will never get what they want because they do not want it enough. They think they want it. They say they want it, but that means little compared to what is required to get it.

As Jim Collins wrote in *Good To Great*, "Few people attain great lives, in large part because it is just so easy to settle for a good life."

That's the case for many people. Their career is good enough. They are successful enough. Their life is good enough.

For those of you who are still ambitious, know that by tapping into your burning desire, the rest of this becomes easy—and not because you will have all the motivation you need for taking action, but because with burning desire, you will unlock all of your resources for getting it.

PERFORMANCE TOOL 1: ACCESSING RESOURCES

Sit back and close your eyes. Put your feet on the floor, your hands on your lap, and sit up straight. Take a breath. Exhale slowly. Take two more breaths, exhaling more slowly each time. Don't just read these words, really take a good ten minutes to use this and the other performance tools.

Think back to a time in your life you had a definite purpose and the burning desire to achieve your goal. See yourself there, think about what inspired you, and notice how you took action. Now, look forward into your future seeing what you want today. Taking this same intensity of desire, what action are you now taking? Now, commit to take it!

— **2** —

THE FIRST RULE OF MIND CONTROL

Any thought *not* moving you toward what you want is moving you further away, so choose only the thoughts that cause you to take action and move forward.

You do that by using my first rule of mind control: Only think about what you want. That means: Stop thinking about what you do *not* want and orient every single thought (really, every. single. thought.) to what you do want. Think about that. Any limitations you have had can be re-oriented to focus on what you want and the actions you can take to get it.

An example of this thinking was provided by Seahawks quarterback Russell Wilson in his post-game interview after leading his team to a crushing victory in Super Bowl XLVIII: "I remember my dad asking me one time, and it's something that has always stuck with me: 'Why not you, Russ?'

"You know, why not me? Why not me in the Super Bowl? So in speaking to our football team earlier in the year, I said, 'Why not us? Why can't we be there?'"

PERFORMANCE TOOL 2: MINDSET PROGRAMMING

Russell Wilson's phrase, "why not you?" is an example of an auto-suggestion. To use this performance tool, create a list of your own auto-suggestions, which you read daily for training your thinking. Be sure to infuse your auto-suggestions with emotion and the sense that by taking actions you are already on your way to getting what you want.

To optimize this performance tool, find ways to broadcast your programming. Put reminders on your desk. Stick motivational quotes on your wall. Record for yourself ideas you listen to over and over again. Whatever it takes, constantly program your thinking.

3

HACK YOUR MIND AND BODY

The secret to choosing your thinking is to recognize that any thought you have in your mind can be changed to any thought you want.

If you have, for instance, a voice in your head that says: *I am a loser*, change it! Just like you would stop listening to an awful song on the radio, be like those people who cut you off and interrupt when you are speaking. Change the message and the messenger by changing the voice and the thought.

The same is true with pictures in your head. If you feel bad when you look at awful pictures on the news, stop watching. Do you have awful pictures in your head? Change it. If you are imagining yourself failing worse than a drunk man impaling himself on a fence, replace it with a positive image.

I know that sounds overly simple, but it really is that simple. Do it and see!

Another simple way to change your thinking is to hack your body. As you know, your thoughts drive your feelings and your feelings drive your actions in a cycle, and by changing your body posture, you can drive your thoughts.

PERFORMANCE TOOL 3:

PRACTICE YOUR POSTURE AND THINKING

Watch Amy Cuddy's TED talk on body language, and you can learn a number of postures that will trigger certain feelings. Practice hacking your mind and body for a few minutes regularly during the day: Stand akimbo—like Superman, with your hands on your hips and elbows bowed out—and create pictures and thoughts in your mind that get you feeling like Superman. Then see yourself taking powerful actions and getting what you want.

—— 4 ——

LIMITLESS IMAGINATION

What distinguished Albert Einstein was his astounding ability to use his mind and, in particular, his imagination. In fact, one of his most famous thought experiments was imagining himself riding on a beam of light tunneling through the universe. This daydream contributed to his revolutionary theory of relativity. In this sense, it was not just intelligence that set him apart, but the way he could bend his mind.

Steve Jobs once said: "Life can be much broader once you discover one simple fact. That everything around you they call life was made up by people that were no smarter than you. And you can change it, you can influence it, you can build things other people can use."

Whatever you want your career and life to be, it begins with you first imagining it to be possible. It's that simple.

PERFORMANCE TOOL 4: VISUALIZATION

Next time you watch Phil Mickelson step up to the tee, imagine what is going through his mind. Standing over the tee, as he grips the club, looking down at the ball and ahead to the fairway he is visualizing his perfect shot.

Do the same for your career. Like you dreamed as a child, imagine unleashing your limitless imagination in the direction of the career and life you truly want. As often as you can, sit back, close your eyes, and imagine your career and life unfolding as you desire. Take at least ten minutes to do this, and just for fun, imagine for a day acting as if it has already happened.

5

BUILD POWERFUL BELIEFS

Henry Ford famously mused, "Whether you think you can, or think you cannot, you are right." You will only take actions when your beliefs are strong.

Have you ever been at a circus and seen an elephant, the world's most powerful land creature, tethered by a small rope attached to a weak wooden spike nailed in the ground? If it tried, the elephant could clearly break free.

So why doesn't it try? Because at a young age, when a baby elephant joins the circus, she is tethered with a strong chain attached to a metal spike cemented in the ground. No matter how hard she tugs, the baby elephant cannot break free. As a baby, she learns to stop trying.

The same heartbreaking tale is true for humans. Early in life we believe anything is possible, yet over time, we become conditioned to believe our options are limited.

Unlike elephants, we have the power to recognize and then change our beliefs, choosing the beliefs that get us to take powerful actions.

PERFORMANCE TOOL 5: WRITE THE SCRIPT

Your beliefs are one hundred percent formed by the stories you tell yourself. Rather than telling yourself crappy stories of what is not possible, craft powerful stories of how by taking the actions you are on your way to getting what you want. Begin every day with an exercise I call morning glory: Spend ten minutes telling yourself (aloud) the story of the career and life you truly want and the steps you are now taking to get it.

6

LIMITLESS "YOU"

Born in 1904, Archibald Leach was the son of an abusive alcoholic who abandoned Archibald and his mother. At age ten, Archibald's life got even worse when he came home to discover his mother had gone missing. Without either parent, and not knowing what to do, he made a bold decision.

He imagined the person he would grow to be, and he resolved to become that "character." Years later, he said, "I pretended to be somebody I wanted to be, and I finally became that person, or he became me."

In that way, regular Archibald Leach became the legendary Cary Grant.

That is the concept of building a limitless "you." Rather than seeing yourself for who you are today, see yourself for who you choose to be, and take the actions to become that person.

PERFORMANCE TOOL 6: BUILD YOUR SELF-IMAGE

Written in 1960 by former plastic surgeon Maxwell Maltz, *Psycho Cybernetics* succinctly identifies an often over-looked aspect of all success and achievement. In *Psycho Cybernetics*, Maltz concluded that success is driven by two things: First, you must be able to visualize a positive outcome. Second, you must adopt the self-image that is consistent with achieving your outcome. Practice rehearsing your ideal self-image until it becomes "you."

7

REHEARSE SUCCESS

Perhaps the greatest master on personal change to have ever lived, Dr. Milton Erickson said, "You can pretend anything and master it." A way to do this is through mental rehearsal.

In a famous study of basketball players, researchers learned that those who did zero practice but only mentally rehearsed shooting hoops performed almost as well as those who took shots for practice.

For every shot Michael Jordan sunk, every ball Tiger Woods hit, every stroke Michael Phelps took, they practiced many times over in their minds. In fact, Phelps attributes mental rehearsal as his secret to earning fifteen Olympic Gold medals. Since seven years old, Phelps has spent each night before bed watching the "videotape" of his perfect swim.

PERFORMANCE TOOL 7: MENTAL REHEARSAL

For hours on end Michael Jordan would sit back and imagine himself sinking shot after shot. Imagining activating the same muscles, he would see himself jumping and gracefully releasing the ball through his fingertips.

You too can use mental rehearsal daily for everything you do. To an extreme, I used this tool to "cure" a client of performance anxiety he was suffering ahead of big meetings. By training him to sit back, close his eyes, and imagine his meetings playing out perfectly, he restored his confidence, taking him back to the top of his game.

—— **8** ——

TRAIN ENERGY AND FOCUS

Success takes energy. And success in a hard-charging career takes a lot of energy. The long hours, early mornings, late nights, intense focus, travel, and client entertainment are often part of the package. Just to keep up takes a lot of energy.

As importantly, your physical energy also drives your emotional energy. When you watch someone stroll into a room charismatically, bringing positivity and enthusiasm with him, the energy is more than physical. His emotional energy drives success.

While your physical and emotional energy is of course driven by a number of complex factors—and I encourage you to focus carefully on exercise, sleep, and nutrition—it is also important to recognize how your thinking affects your energy.

It is said that one hour of thinking is the equivalent of ten minutes of kick-boxing, and you can reclaim your energy by thinking more efficiently—stop worrying and thinking about other useless stuff—and training your focus on the now.

Not only will focus improve your energy, but it is also paramount to success. In *The Snowball*, a biography of Warren Buffett, Alice Schroeder recounts a story of Bill Gates, Sr. asking, "What factor did you feel was the most important in getting to where you've gotten in life?"

"Focus," replied Buffett.

PERFORMANCE TOOL 8: TRAIN YOUR FOCUS

While the doctors jacking up our kids on speed might suggest otherwise, training focus is easy. The best tool is meditation, but you can train your focus simply by limiting task-switching and training your mind to stop wandering. Albert Einstein would keep a pen and pad next to him when he read. Every time his mind wandered, even for an instant, he would mark his pad. Then he would say silently to himself, "I won't be distracted by that again." He apparently reached forty-two minutes of un-interrupted focus!

9

GET IN THE FLOW

Dale Carnegie said, "Success is getting what you want. Happiness is wanting what you get." Getting what you want is happiness and success!

Too many of us are striving continuously trying to get "somewhere," hoping when we someday reach our elusive definition of success, it will be everything we imagine it to be.

But, if you don't already feel successful or happy with what you have achieved, how will any more success change that? It won't. The only solution is choosing the thinking that feels amazing today and everyday.

I discovered the secret to doing this years ago when I left Los Angeles and was living in Vail skiing. Every day, I skied until my legs burned. Challenging myself and loving it, I wondered: *How can your career feel the same way?*

The trick is to get beyond striving to get "somewhere," and become absorbed in loving what you are doing every day.

Even if you don't love what you do, you can love the feeling of being fully engaged in a task. Like being in the middle of a great run, when you have stopped thinking and you are fully absorbed in the moment, you reach a peak experience known as *flow*. The same as an athlete being "in the zone," flow is not only a peak state for performance, it is also a peak experience for happiness.

PERFORMANCE TOOL 9: PRACTICE FLOW

In the definitive book on flow, aptly titled *Flow*, Mihaly Csikszentmihalyi gives us a formula for achieving flow. He says there are three primary conditions:

1. You must have a goal.

2. You must have a feedback mechanism.

3. The perceived challenge of the task must be consistent with your skill level—that is, if the task is too easy, you get bored; if it is too hard, you get discouraged.

Practice this guide. It is built for flow!

10

EVOLVE!

The previous thinking and tools are like hitting the gym and getting into great shape, but the evolutionary tools take you to a new level altogether.

In Maslow's Hierarchy of Needs, the steps up the pyramid escalate from basic human needs to overcoming physical and emotional needs to the ideal of self-actualization at the top of the pyramid.

Well, the evolutionary tools take you beyond Maslow's limited pyramid! They enable you to advance yourself as a human being and then keep advancing yourself beyond the basic mind/body experience.

Now, if you are concerned that these ideas are a little woo-woo, good! If you want to evolve beyond the meat-and-two-veg, you must get a little woo-woo.

PERFORMANCE TOOL 10: THE EVOLUTIONARY TOOLS

I am writing a book on evolutionary tools, and I cannot overemphasize the power of these tools for creating the life you truly want. For now, I simply suggest you consider exploring:

1. PRACTICING MEDITATION. An easy way to start is by downloading the app Headspace.

2. TRAINING AWARENESS. An excellent tool for training is *Open Focus*, which is a downloadable program by Les Fehmi of The Princeton Biofeedback Center.

3. TRAINING YOUR BRAINWAVES. Like music jacks you into a certain way of feeling, explore brainwave entrainment programs. Start simply: Search online for free binaural beats.

4. LEARNING THE MOST POWERFUL EVOLUTIONARY TOOLS: hypnosis and Neuro-linguistic Programming (NLP).

Some people use these tools simply for stress relief and whatnot, which is like using your Ferrari for picking up the groceries: they are built for much more. These tools are by far the most powerful tools I have discovered for training your limitless mind, building you into who you choose to be, and propelling you toward getting what you want.

So, evolve and get what you want!

THE PROCESS

The final step to training your limitless mind is developing a process for mental training. Analogous to a program you might use for training your body at the gym, your process is a simple way for you to continue practicing choosing your thinking and applying the tools.

To develop your process, I suggest going back through this section and identifying the thinking you want to keep training and the tools that work best for you. Then I recommend creating three processes:

1. CONTINUOUS PRACTICES: These are the tools you practice all day every day.

2. DAILY PRACTICES: Practice these tools every morning and night.

3. WEEKLY PRACTICES: Practice these tools weekly.

Although this might sound extreme, like consistently exercising and watching your nutrition, you will soon notice mind-blowing transformational results.

PART 2:

THE SYSTEM FOR DOING WHAT YOU WANT!

CHAPTER FIVE

THE SYSTEM FOR DOING WHAT YOU WANT!

First, have a definite, clear practical ideal; a goal, an objective. Second, have the necessary means to achieve your ends; wisdom, money, materials, and methods. Third, adjust all your means to that end.

— ARISTOTLE

★　　★　　★　　★　　★　　★

Imagine that you are an ambitious career-type with the goal of running your company. (That might sound grandiose, but as long as you have a system for doing what you want, why not apply it to a grand goal?)

The goal is clear: You will run your company. You have definite purpose.

Now, how do you next develop *Your System for Doing What You Want?*

This is what you will learn in the following chapters. As a reminder, here is the complete *System*:

1. FIRST, YOU *DEFINE IT*, meaning that you change the orientation of your goal by defining it as a process. Rather than saying your goal is to run your company, you say that your goal is to create *Your System* that leads to the result of running your company.

   With that slight change in orientation, you have gone from a results-based (and therefore abstract) goal to a clearly defined process-related goal that has concrete steps.

2. IN *GETTING IT*, you will figure out how to pull it off. What must you do and who must you become to successfully execute your process of running your company? Here, you will research role models and models of success, build your intelligence through the principles, and then create a custom-fitted strategy for you and your career.

3. IN *PLAN IT*, you will take your ideas from the first two steps and build your plan by breaking down your goal into three separate workstreams:

   • EXTERNAL: the steps required to drive commercial success.

   • INTERNAL: the steps to get support inside your company.

   • DEVELOPMENT: who you must become to run your company.

4. AS THIS STEP, *EXECUTE IT*, implies, you are executing your plan.

In this step, you actually iterate back and forth between *Plan It* and *Execute It*, constantly working and re-working your plan as you keep moving toward getting what you want.

5.   NEXT, YOU ARE *GETTING SKILLS*, meaning you will develop the skills you need for executing your process and getting what you want.

For instance, in executing your internal and external workstreams, you may decide to step up your skill of communication. To have more impact in less time, you might improve your skill of time management. What about the skill of mindset? The skill of selling? What other skills do you need to develop in reaching your goal of running your company? Having assessed the skills you need, you will develop your process of learning, quickly developing the skills you need for getting what you want.

Putting all these steps together, you will build *Your System for Doing What You Want!* Then, over time, you will simply keep working *Your System* through a process of continuously improving the steps you take in moving toward your goal.

Now, of course that's just one example of how you might apply *The System for Doing What You Want!,* and as you'll see in the next section, *The System* is designed to be incredibly flexible to work with whatever goals you choose.

CHAPTER SIX

DEFINE IT

I knew when I was eighty that I would never, for example, think about why I walked away from my 1994 Wall Street bonus right in the middle of the year at the worst possible time. That kind of thing just isn't something you worry about when you're eighty years old.

— JEFF BEZOS, *THE EVERYTHING STORE*

★ ★ ★ ★ ★ ★

You do not need to read book after book or study after study to know that setting goals is important to getting what you want. If you are firing a gun, you already know that you damn well better have a target.

Yet, few of us set goals. Even the smart and successful people I know rarely set goals. Most are head down, pounding away. Like lumberjacks successfully chopping wood, we are often unclear if we are even in the right forest.

Most of us are never taught how to set goals. From an early age, most goals are set for us: Get good grades, then go to college, then get a good job.

And let's face it: Most approaches to goal setting are completely useless in today's modern world, where the only certainty is enormous uncertainty.

Beyond that lies a much, much more challenging reason few of us set goals. We get stuck before we get started. We simply do not know what we want.

While that sounds like bad news, here is the good news. In fact, this is revolutionary news...

You do not need to know exactly what you want.

I was grinding away for the better part of ten years trying to figure out what I wanted, and I believed that if only I could figure out what I wanted, then I could get it.

But I was wrong!

Here's the secret: In *The System for Doing What You Want!* you do not need to know exactly what you want, you need only to keep defining your process so that you can keep moving in the right direction. I know this sounds nuts, but in this section, I will show you how to get what you want— even if you do not know what that is.

SETTING THE TARGET

In this step, we define your goal, which sets you up for all the other steps of *The System.*

1
DEFINE
IT

In *Define It, you* will define your goal in a way that is unlike traditional approaches to goal setting. These methods focus on your goal as an outcome, but in *Define It,* you define your goal as a process.

Let us use the weightlifter example. Lifting a world-record weight is certainly a great goal, but it is different from defining a goal. Lifting a heavy bar stacked with weights is a desired outcome, but a defined goal for a weightlifter is: Developing the process of building myself into the person who can lift a world-record weight.

In *Define It,* the *process* is your goal.

Although you will target the same outcome, stating your goal as a process immediately puts you into motion.

It is action-oriented because it assumes movement. You can set a goal of driving your career to the top and have that goal exist as some floating ideal that you somehow, someday, some way might perhaps achieve. But when you define your goal as the process of driving your career to the top, you are already called to take action.

Setting your goal as a process also means that even if you are lacking definite purpose for what you want, you can have definite purpose for your process of getting it.

For instance, let's say that you don't know whether you want to stay on your current career track or make a move. In this case you lack definite purpose for your desired outcome, but it is still easy for you to have definite purpose in your process for driving your career forward toward either outcome.

A SOPHISTICATED APPROACH

Henry Ford said, "The whole secret of a successful life is to find out what is one's destiny to do, and then do it."

Practically, this means, dreaming up your destiny and then working backward by identifying the steps you must take to get there. This is something traditional goal-setting frameworks fail to help you do.

Traditional goal-setting frameworks, such as the SMART system, are excellent for tackling short-term, well-defined goals, but they fail to orient you toward your more abstract long-term goals. Conversely, goal-setting frameworks that ask you to set big, hairy goals are good for stretching your potential, but they are too abstract to give you a path for getting there.

You either miss the forest for the trees, or you miss the trees for the forest!

The ideal approach is one that combines the two, locking you onto the grandest vision for your career and also keeping you focused on the steps you take to get there. That alone is a powerful formula. But it isn't enough.

Earlier, we talked about the problem many of us face in not knowing what we want. And there's a bigger problem: By nature, your career is volatile. We all face a huge amount of uncertainty.

So unlike traditional goal-setting approaches, which often analogize your goals to building a house, where all variables are fixed and determinable, you need an approach that recognizes that few of the inputs and outputs of your goals are fixed and determinable. You require a sophisticated framework built for navigating the complexity, volatility, and uncertainty of your career.

Putting all this together by building in short-term and long-term planning and a process for navigating uncertainty, *Define It* works in these four steps:

1. FIRST, you orient toward a concrete or abstract vision of what you want. (I call this the "grandest vision for your career.")

2. SECOND, using a specific framework that navigates uncertainty, you develop your roadmap.

3. NEXT, you apply a more traditional approach to setting your clearly-definable goals.

4. AND, FINALLY, you *Define It,* establishing your goals as a process.

CHAPTER SEVEN

— STEP 1 —

WHAT DO YOU WANT?

Sometimes the questions are complicated and the answers are simple.

— DR. SEUSS

★　　★　　★　　★　　★　　★

The typical advice for goal setting is well captured by Yogi Berra:

"You've got to be very careful if you don't know where you're going, because you might not get there."

It seems like good advice, but it's wrong—and thank God for that!

If you do not know what you want, it is not for lack of trying. Believe me, I learned this lesson the hard way.

For almost ten years, I had this conversation:

ME: *What do I want?*

ME: *I don't know.*

ME: *How can you not know?*

ME: *I don't know.*

ME: *You really need to figure that out.*

ME: *Yes, okay, so what do I want?*

ME: *I don't know?*

ME: *How can you not know?*

And so the cycle continued. For years, like a circular reference #REF!'g out, I asked the same question over and over, getting no closer to an answer, only grinding my gears.

I felt even more confused with almost every book I read. These books, mostly written for those aspiring, assumed that I wanted "to be successful," but they gave no intelligent approach to figuring out what "success" meant for me.

As I discovered in my research, it's hard to know what you want.

I know people in their seventies who say, "I don't know what I want when I grow up." And the bizarre truth about happiness is that research suggests that we do not know what has made us happy in the past, let alone what will make us happy in the future!

Compounding matters is this: We live in a time of great choice. While a gift, being bombarded with choice is also a curse as we find it harder to choose among the many options available. We find ourselves stuck in decision pa-ralysis, fearful of regretting the choices we don't make.

Making choices can be hard, and in a modern career it can be much harder. There is no such thing as a job for life and throughout your career you are blessed and cursed with choice. Do you keep doing what you are doing? Change companies? Do something different?

For your entire career, you are presented with difficult choices that demand you figure out what you want.

★ ★ ★ ★ ★ ★

THE DIRTY SECRET

While over the years I felt lost and struggled to figure out what I wanted, in hindsight I realized I had been on track all along. Whereas for years I struggled to figure out what I wanted, looking back I saw, even though I did not know what I wanted, by continuing to take action and advance in the right direction, I was simply figuring it out over time.

THE DIRTY SECRET:

To get what you want you don't need to know what you want!

That's right! To get what you want, you do not need to know what you want. You only need to define a process that keeps you moving in the right direction.

Truth be told, questions like, "What's the meaning of life?" and "What do I want?" are an intellectual wank. There is no answer to, "What do I want?" It's simply a question you answer at different points in time.

Think about it this way: Have you ever gotten something you wanted—like a promotion or a lover—and thought: *Well, that's it. I can die satisfied now.*

Not a chance!

When you graduated college and got your first job, did you stop wanting? How about when you bought your first car or house?

Of course not. In those instances, getting what you wanted was just your stepping stone to the next thing you wanted.

"What do you want?" is not a question you need to answer, but is the question you are living. There is no answer. There is only your journey of the question, as you keep moving forward honoring your "wants" over time.

This means even if you cannot clearly define what you ultimately want, as long as you can keep dreaming of the type of career you want and stay focused on the next "want" right in front of you, you can keep defining your process and next steps for getting there.

Like an explorer who sets out will not know where he will eventually land, you keep moving forward anyway, answering your questions along the way and changing courses when you have more clarity.

Think of it by using Jack Canfield's analogy in *The Secret:* The process of living your goals is like driving a car at night. Your headlights might light up only two hundred feet in front of your car, but you can drive from California to New York by navigating what is right ahead, allowing the road to unfold in front of you.

You do this in your career by recognizing that no matter where you are headed, you will get there from where you are sitting right now. Therefore, by continually redefining your process and lighting up the goals in front of you, you keep moving toward your grandest vision.

*   *   *   *   *   *

THE SECRET IS TO KEEP MOVING FORWARD

Not knowing what you want is only a problem when you are so stuck in indecision that you fail to get anywhere. This is a common problem for many of us, as James Altucher wrote in *Choose Yourself*, "The most popular question I get via e-mail is 'I'm stuck. How can I move forward in life?'"

An early client of mine was an investment banker contemplating retirement. Having spent more than a year thinking through his decision and drawing up decision trees and lists of pros and cons, he found himself stuck, unable to decide.

While on the surface, his problem was not knowing whether to stay or leave, his problem actually happened before that.

His problem was that in being stuck at the decision point, he was not committed to either choice: staying and succeeding or retiring and getting on with his life.

Theodore Roosevelt once said, "In a moment of decision, the best thing you can do is the right thing to do. The worst thing you can do is nothing."

The same is true in your career. The worst thing you can do is remain at the decision point, thereby failing to commit to any choice and getting nowhere as a result!

Today, perhaps more than any time in human history, many people are searching for their passion. Yet, by looking for it somewhere outside of themselves or hoping their passion will one day magically appear, they fail to see passion is something that comes from inside you and is developed through purposeful action.

Rather than seeing—*What do I want?*—as a question you must answer, see it as a question you will allow yourself to realize over time by taking action and moving forward.

But that doesn't mean you just keep your head down and keep powering forward. In fact, the opposite is true.

★   ★   ★   ★   ★   ★

BEGIN WITH THE END IN MIND

You have two choices for setting the direction of your career.

You can begin where you are today, looking forward to the steps right in front of you. Or, as I encourage, you can start by beginning with the end in mind, at the grandest vision for your career, and looking backward on the steps you can take to get there.

Once again, this doesn't mean you need to know exactly where you are headed. You only need to be able to dream up a grand vision for your career and stay focused on the steps in front of you that keep you moving there.

For instance, although you might not know today whether you want to be in your current job five years from now, beginning with the end in mind, you can see what truly matters—taking the steps forward today that keep you moving toward your dream career and life.

As Stephen Covey writes on his Habit 2: Begin With The End In Mind, "It means to know where you're going so that you better understand where you are now and so that the steps you take are always in the right direction."

Beginning with the end in mind is also important because, as Michelangelo said, "The greater danger for most of us lies not in setting our aim too high and falling short; but in setting our aim too low, and achieving our mark."

This is the danger in only looking forward from today. From your current job, you are more likely to think "realistically." Shrouded by a limited mindset or limited choices, doing what you truly want might seem unrealistic, so you risk setting your sights on what seems possible rather than going for what you truly want.

By beginning with the end in mind, you're focused on what you truly want, which gets you excited, which gets you thinking about all the ways it is possible, which gets you moving in the right direction, which makes it possible. Even if you can't clearly define what you want, by setting your sights on a vision for your career and life that you love, you are taking actions and moving forward.

And even if you never reach that goal, as Norman Vincent Peale put it, "Shoot for the moon because even if you miss, you'll land among the stars."

EXERCISE

WHAT DO YOU WANT?

By beginning with the end in mind, you can give yourself the freedom to dream up the grandest vision for your career.

Forget about realistic goals and develop your Big Hairy Audacious Goals (BHAGs) that Jim Collins and Jerry Porras describe in *Built to Last.* By all means, get unrealistic. Get stupid.

We spend our entire lives being careful and setting limits. Think far beyond what is possible or probable or likely from where you are sitting, and just dream up what you truly want.

I don't know what that is for you, but I do know that deep down each of us has a vision for what we truly want. Ever since I was a kid, I dreamed to live a life of freedom and do what I want every day. I had no idea what that meant or how I would do it, but it is the vision that guides me. I'm certain you too have a vision of what constitutes the grandest vision for your career and life.

Give yourself zero room for modesty. Refuse to insulate yourself from failure. Stop yourself from thinking things like—*Oh, that's never going to happen.* Instead, think as big and bold as you can imagine, then establish the most exciting vision you have for your career. Remember, as Zig Ziglar said, "If you can dream it, you can achieve it."

One of my former bosses once suggested that I imagine floating above my own funeral listening to my eulogy being read.

Sure, it's a little morbid, but when all is said and done, what would you like to hear people say about your career? Your life?

If this doesn't help you set BHAGs, try stepping into another great person's shoes. For a moment, see the world through the eyes of someone like Columbus, Roosevelt, Lincoln, or Henry Ford. What did they dream of? What about Elon Musk who dreamed to put a rocket in space? Or Jeff Bezos, who dreamed to build the everything store?

Do this now, right now. Don't just read these black letters on the white page. Take a moment to close your eyes and dream in vivid color.

Relax. Put your feet on the floor. Rest your arms comfortably in your lap.

Take a deep breath and slowly exhale. Do this two more times, each time noticing your mind slowing down.

Now close your eyes and imagine the boldest vision for your career. Are you retiring early and sitting on the beach? Do you see yourself rising all the way to the top? Are you leaving your current career and doing something else? Are you already far beyond that point, dreaming bigger?

See it unfolding now. See yourself in five, ten, twenty, thirty years. What are you doing? Who are you spending your life with? What type of career and life are you living? What is the meaning of the life you have lived?

Now imagine yourself sitting in an IMAX theater and watching the boldest vision for your career playing on the biggest screen. How can you turn it up even more? How can you make it bigger? Bolder? More real?

Having enjoyed that for a while, imagine stepping into your movie at the end and looking back to the you who is sitting in your seat right now. From that vantage point, imagine seeing the steps you have taken to create your grandest vision for your career.

Now, having gone all the way to the end and looked back on the steps you might take to create your grandest vision of your career, imagine looking forward and seeing just the one next step for you to take.

Sit with that for a moment, and imagine taking it, then the next, and the next, and the next steps, over years building the grandest vision you have for your career.

Now, ask yourself. What do you get from taking the actions and creating your grandest vision for your career? What word or picture or feeling do you get? And what do you get from having that? And having that? And having that? And having that? How inspired do you now feel to take the actions for creating the career and life you truly want?

Now. Come back to the desert of the real and reflect on what you got from doing this exercise. I suggest repeating this exercise every day for the next ten days. If you are serious about doing what you want, on Day 10, write a script for your grandest vision. Then record this script and listen to it over and over again, continually dreaming of the career and life you are creating.

That's it for Step 1. That's all we are doing here: getting you set up thinking right about your long-term, grandest vision for your career and thinking about how your steps will take you there.

CHAPTER EIGHT

=== STEP 2 ===

THE ROADMAP

Yes, there are two paths you can go by, but in the long run,
there's still time to change the road you're on.

— LED ZEPPELIN, "STAIRWAY TO HEAVEN"

★ ★ ★ ★ ★ ★

Now that you are imagining creating the career you truly want, you can start mapping all the ways for getting there.

The Roadmap not only gives you a framework for defining your short and long-term goals, it also helps you navigate the choice and uncertainty of your career. In essence, you lay out the potential tracks for getting what you want.

And keep in mind: You do not yet need to see all your steps. You only need to see that your roadmap contains the next steps that are moving you in the right direction toward the grandest vision for your career.

As author Gloria Steinem said, "Dreaming, after all, is a form of planning."

Think of your roadmap in the same way you might plan a road trip. You would have in mind your ultimate destination, and sitting down looking at a roadmap, depending on how long you want to take and the type of adventure you want to have, you can see the many different ways you might get there.

The pivotal steps and turning points in your career can be considered in the same way. What leads to the next steps? Over what timeframes? All of these answers will give you a better context for the steps you will take from here.

Another benefit of this perspective is that you can unlock new ways of thinking about your career. There's an age-old question of whether to follow your heart or get a "good" job, but in looking at your roadmap, you will see that you never have to answer that question. Instead, you can experience different types of jobs at different points in your life, having both "good" jobs (or what I call objective-based jobs) and passion-based jobs over the course of a long career. It is all merely a matter of the type of adventure you want to have.

However you think about it, in looking forward from where you are, imagine all the different paths that might lead you to doing what you truly want. Now, having visualized the ways your career might play out, let's get more specific in developing your roadmap.

★ ★ ★ ★ ★ ★

DEVELOPING YOUR DUAL-TRACK ROADMAP

In beginning with the end in mind, you focused on creating your grandest vision for the career you truly want. Now, in developing your roadmap, you are conceptualizing the different tracks you might take to get there.

Here is the trick: As much as your career involves great uncertainty, the truth is that you have only two choices or tracks for your career.

On one track, your status-quo track, you keep driving forward in your current career. On the other, your alternative track, you take a different path.

Though many people get overwhelmed by their choices, in fact, these are the only two tracks that require your focus in driving your career. No matter where you are headed, there are only these two ways of getting there.

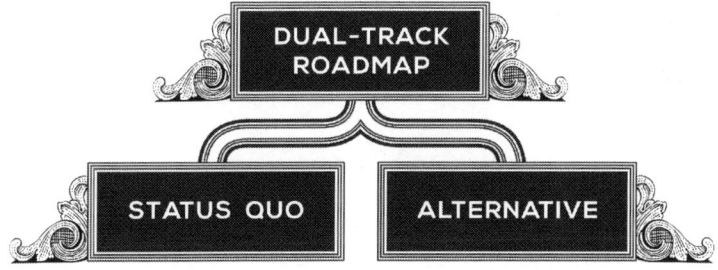

To keep moving forward in creating the career you truly want, you only need to be focused on driving your status-quo track (from which all your other options are created), and at the right points in time, evaluate your alternatives for making moves and taking a different track.

Consider my friend who is an associate principal at McKinsey & Company with the BHAG to one day start her own company. Beginning with that idea, you can imagine that there are many ways of getting there. On her status-quo track, she might stay in consulting for many years before setting off on her own. Or, alternatively she might first make a move to a corporate gig, which might help set her up to start her own company down the track.

With these ideas in mind, you lay out your dual-track roadmap.

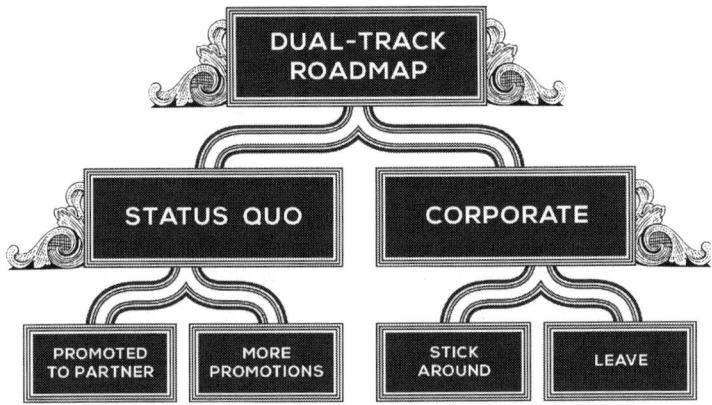

So even though she is not sure when she will leave to start her own company, or whether she will first make a move to the corporate-side, her dual-track roadmap gives her a simple way to keep moving forward in her current career while also exploring her alternatives.

Seeing your career this way, your choice becomes clear. Unless you are today, right now, committed to pursuing one of your alternative tracks, you are committed to the step right in front of you on your status-quo track. So no matter whether you know exactly what you want, your choice is clear: focus on crushing your current career track, knowing all of your options keep unfolding from there.

★ ★ ★ ★ ★ ★

THE POWER OF COMMITMENT

Using your dual-track roadmap relieves the pressure to clearly define what you want because, irrespective of where your career is headed, by focusing on the track right in front you, you are already moving in the right direction.

Hence, even if you are unclear of where you are headed, as Ryan Holiday writes in *The Obstacle Is the Way*, "the obstacle in the path becomes the path."

Rather than getting stuck with choices, trying to decide whether to do one thing or the other, by committing to the step that is right in front of you, you are powerfully moving forward.

This is important in your career in the same way it is important in the classic arcade game *Frogger*. If you are not moving, you are street-kill. You have little time to stand idle in your career, so as you land in one place, you must be looking for your next leap.

Doing what you want in your career requires that type of commitment from you. In fact, because of the way the dual-track roadmap is designed, your commitment is made explicit. The danger of being stuck at any decision point—say contemplating whether to stay or leave—is that you fail to commit to either track.

But your dual-track roadmap simply and concretely eliminates decision paralysis. Looking down your dual-track roadmap, you see that when you are committed to your current track, you are laying the groundwork for exploring other options. Indeed, moving forward in your current track is essential to success wherever you might go.

Unfortunately, that's where many people fail.

You know those people. They are neither two feet in nor two feet out, instead spending their careers on uneven footing, neither committing to success in their current seat nor committing to leaving. I am sure you know some people who have spent the bulk of their careers that way.

Avoid being like them. These people inevitably become mid-tier performers, easily out-performed by those who are committed to being the best they can be.

In contrast, those who run the dual-track roadmap are both committed to success in their current seat and to evaluating other options, setting themselves up to succeed inside or outside their current track.

And if it turns out that you are not headed in the right direction, like steering a car that is already moving, you will have an easier time turning if you are already making strides in your career. With all your forward momentum, you will find it easy to keep making new choices.

★   ★   ★   ★   ★   ★

OFF THE ROADMAP

To some people, the career moves I've made were down-right crazy. A former colleague analogized my career track to abandoning a luxury yacht in the middle of the sea, looking back, and yelling, "It's okay! I'll swim from here!" Then, after getting picked up by another yacht, doing the same thing before turning and swimming farther out to sea. But I saw it differently.

Mark Twain said, "Twenty years from now, you will be more disappointed by the things that you didn't do than by the ones you did do, so throw off the bowlines, sail away from safe harbor, catch the trade winds in your sails. Explore, Dream, Discover."

Fortune's 100 Best Companies to Work For ran a story of Goldman Sachs' Marty Chavez. Today, a member of Goldman's exclusive Management Committee, Chavez has a career track that is anything but conventional. Chavez left Goldman early in his career, and went on to found and sell his own company. While cleaning toilets in a monastery in New Mexico he had a new epiphany for his career.

Realizing he could affect global transformation at Goldman, he returned, making partner a year later and quickly rising from there.

I share his story because when you are in the trenches and focused on your career, it is not always possible to see how stepping out of your day-to-day life might lead to transformational outcomes. Yet, when you begin to think of getting off the roadmap entirely—such as an old friend who left Wall Street to join the Peace Corps—you begin to see not only how many more options are available but also just how far those options might take you.

EXERCISE

YOUR ROADMAP

Take a few moments to think about your roadmap. Imagine your grandest vision for your career. Then begin sketching out your paths for getting there.

Begin with the end in mind, looking back to where you are today. Just for a moment think about all the different ways you can keep moving toward the career and life you truly want.

Now, look forward from where you are. What are the steps right in front of you on your current track? What are the alternative tracks that you can be considering today and at different points in the future? What are the right turning points—e.g., after your next promotion—and the ways you can imagine your alternative tracks playing out?

Take as little or as much time as you want to do this. For some of you it might just be a few boxes on a page and for others it might become a more elaborate series of decision trees for your career. However you do it, what matters is you take the time to map out your future career.

Having done this exercise, keep coming back to it for a few weeks. Really challenge yourself, ask yourself, what is missing? Are you too limited in your thinking? How can you expand on the ways you are evaluating your alternatives to keep creating the career you truly want?

Okay. That's it for *The Roadmap*.

AT THIS POINT, WE ARE SPLITTING OFF AND LEAVING BEHIND THE ALTERNATIVE TRACKS. FOR THE REST OF *DEFINE IT* AND THROUGHOUT THE NEXT FOUR STEPS OF *THE SYSTEM*, WE ARE FOCUSING ON DRIVING YOUR STATUS-QUO TRACK—REMEMBER, NO MATTER WHAT YOU WANT, THE ONLY WAY YOU ARE GETTING THERE IS BY DRIVING YOUR CAREER FROM WHERE YOU ARE RIGHT NOW.

THEN, IN CHAPTER 27: *GETTING OUT*, WE CIRCLE BACK AND FURTHER EXPLORE YOUR ALTERNATIVE TRACKS.

CHAPTER NINE

=== STEP 3 ===

SETTING GOALS

Go confidently in the direction of your dreams. Live the life you have imagined.

— Henry David Thoreau

★　　★　　★　　★　　★　　★

Here, looking ahead on your roadmap, we are getting laser-focused on your status-quo track, adding depth to your plan by defining the specific goal right in front of you.

Going back to our previous example, let's imagine you are my friend at McKinsey & Company evaluating whether you want to continue in consulting or make a move to the corporate-side. In the meantime, still focused on powering forward, you are looking ahead defining your process for getting promoted. With this specific goal in mind, let's focus on the five principles of goal setting.

<hr>

PRINCIPLE 1

A GOAL IS PROCESS, PROCESS, PROCESS

Principle 1 reinforces the core theme of *Define It:* Focus not on outcomes, but on your goal-achieving process.

You do that by getting focused on the process steps that make them happen. Define your goal not as getting promoted, but instead as developing and executing your process to get promoted. Rather than sitting around all day and thinking *I want to get promoted,* spend all day every day taking the steps in your process toward getting promoted.

Again, while defining your goal as a process might sound semantic, it makes a massive difference. For instance, say you are my friend with a dream to start her own company. Defined that way, you will be chasing some pie-in-the-sky idea. But if you define your goal as developing and executing your process to start your own company, you see that what you really need to do is create a plan, and that seems much, much more doable and concrete.

PRINCIPLE 2

A GOAL IS WELL-FORMED

Your goals must be well-formed, meaning:

- First, your goals must be stated in the positive. Rather than focusing on what you don't want (e.g., "I don't want to get over-looked for promotion"), focus on what you do want (e.g., "I am doing what I can to get promoted").

- Second, your goals must have an "evidence procedure." This means that there must be a way of knowing you have achieved your goal. After all, how can you go after a goal that you do not know how to define or achieve? If your goal is, "I want to create more career options," you should create some sort of evidence procedure to clearly define how many and what type of options you are creating.

- The third concept of well-formed goals is that your goals must have "specific procedures." This means that you can identify some of the markers for achieving them. In our goal to get promoted, specific procedures would be: Identifying the people that you need to convince to support you, and the criteria they will use to judge your readiness.

PRINCIPLE 3

A GOAL IS ACTION-ORIENTED

Defining your goal as a well-formed process encourages you to make your goals actionable and action-oriented, meaning they are defined in such a way that you have full responsibility for achieving them.

For instance, rather than setting your goal as, "Them promoting me," set your goal as, "Taking actions in my process to get promoted."

It might sound nuanced, but stated in this action-oriented way, you send your brain a message of: *Better get to work!*

Just try it yourself, now. Fill in the blank and say, "I want to ____." See how passive that feels?

Now say, "I am taking actions that lead to _____." All of a sudden, you feel like you've got work to do, don't you?

Making your goals action-oriented makes your responsibility for your goals explicit. Your brain realizes that it isn't up to "them" to promote you. It's not up to your boss to support you. It's up to you to do everything you can to get your boss supporting you and get yourself promoted.

So, think of that now. If your goal is to get promoted, what else can you be doing? How do you influence your bosses? What actions can you take to make it happen?

PRINCIPLE 4

A GOAL IS MOTIVATING

Powerful goals are based on powerful motivators. This means you understand your goals behind your goals. You do that by asking yourself:

1. *WHAT DO I GET THROUGH ACHIEVING MY GOAL?*

2. *WHY IS MY GOAL IMPORTANT TO ME?*

3. *WHAT DOES SUCCESSFULLY ACHIEVING MY GOAL LEAD TO?*

For instance, you begin by asking what you get from getting promoted. What is it that is important to you?

Go beyond obvious drivers such as success and money, and deeply explore what emotion getting promoted strikes in you. Pride? Achievement? Beyond that, how does getting promoted fit into your grandest vision for your career?

Remember too, as Simon Sinek wrote in *Start with Why*, "All organizations start with WHY, but only the great ones keep their WHY clear year after year." The same must be true for you.

This is important because when you are aligning your goals with your strongest motivators and deepest desires, you automatically infuse your process with definite purpose.

PRINCIPLE 5

A GOAL IS PLANNED OUT

A goal is not a goal unless it is written down and planned out, all the way to the end. Like baking a cake, you must know every process step, from cracking the eggs to smothering the icing.

The Plan is the difference between dreams and goals, and it is the difference between dreamers and those who get what they want. Dreams are vague ideas that you hope one day might happen, but goals are specific, actionable, measurable, planned out, and executed all the way to the end.

CHAPTER TEN

STEP 4

DEFINE IT

If I had an hour to solve a problem and my life depended on it, I would use the first 55 minutes determining the proper question to ask, for once I knew the proper question, I could solve the problem in less than five minutes.

— ALBERT EINSTEIN

★   ★   ★   ★   ★   ★

In the previous sections, we've been focused on developing a process for laying out what you want and bringing definite purpose to your career. In the first two steps, we were abstract, going from how you figure out what you want to developing the dual-track roadmap where you laid out your status-quo and alternative tracks. In the last step (Setting Goals), we got significantly more specific, adding deliberate process to the goal right in front of you.

Now, we are ready for the fourth and final step: *Define It.* In this step, you will divide and conquer and then create a timeline.

★ ★ ★ ★ ★ ★

DIVIDE AND CONQUER

In divide and conquer, you take the goal in front of you and divide it into the different workstreams that you must manage for getting what you want.

Here's what I mean.

Going back to our example of getting promoted, you divide and conquer by dividing your goal into the separate workstreams that you must manage for successfully getting promoted: External, Internal, You!

Your external workstream is commercial success. No matter what Jedi mind tricks I teach my clients to influence their bosses, what matters most is that you have delivered the commercial success that justifies your promotion.

Your internal workstream is everything you must do inside your company. That means: Who do you need to influence and how do you influence them?

The third workstream relates not to what you must do, but instead to who you must be. More specifically, this workstream specifies how you will develop yourself into the person capable of getting promoted.

★　　★　　★　　★　　★　　★

TIMELINE IT

Having now gone through the process of divide and conquer, you take your workstream goals and break them down according to order and sequence. This doesn't need to be an elaborate step. You need only to think about your goal as it lays out on a timeline.

To do that, I suggest you think of your goals according to three timeframes.

1. THE FIRST TIMEFRAME is right now. That is what you must be doing right if you are to achieve your goals.

   For example, to get promoted, on your external workstream you must be driving your business (whatever that might mean in your career). That requires, right now, ensuring you are focused on the right things and developing your plan to succeed.

2. THE SECOND TIMEFRAME is the next six to twelve months. On this timeline, you are asking yourself: *What must I be doing to reach my year-end goals?*

   For example, on your internal workstream you might recognize that you need to improve your positioning inside your firm and also better "broadcast" your successes. On your timeline you might develop your process for influencing your bosses.

3. THE FINAL TIMEFRAME is the next two to three years, which is a good medium-term cycle in most careers. On this timeline you are asking yourself: *What must I be doing to keep advancing in my career?*

For example, on your You! workstream, you must clearly define who you need to become if you are to be worthy of promotion. Evaluating yourself and your skills on this timeline you would lay out your process of development for building yourself into the person who can achieve your goal.

★ ★ ★ ★ ★ ★

PUTTING IT TOGETHER

Joining your timeline with the tasks that you divided (so that you can conquer them), you might create a summary table like this one:

	Now	6-12 Mos	2-3 Yrs
EXTERNAL	DRIVING BUSINESS		
INTERNAL		INFLUENCING INTERNALLY	
YOU!			NEW YOU!

Can you see how much we have achieved in *Define It*?

Beginning all the way back with figuring out what you want and defining your grandest vision for your career, we have narrowed our focus to the goal right in front of you, developed the workstreams, and timelined a process that keeps you powerfully moving forward in your career.

You can see from here how quickly you could begin to flesh out your goals in a spreadsheet or project management software, laying out the steps you are taking over time on your different workstreams as well as exploring the other alternatives on your dual track.

We will dive deeply into this topic in *Plan It,* but for now, *Define It* serves as preparation for the next chapter, *Getting It.* There we are filling in the pieces, developing the intelligence required for developing your plan, and driving your career.

CHAPTER ELEVEN

GETTING IT

Nothing should be as favorably regarded as intelligence; nothing should be as generously rewarded as intelligence.

— SUN TZU

★　★　★　★　★　★

You hear it all the time:

- "SHE JUST GETS IT."
- "HE DOESN'T GET IT."
- "THEY'LL NEVER GET IT."

While it is obvious whether someone is getting it, what does "getting it" actually mean?

If you walk your office and ask everyone you pass for tips on what it means to be "getting it," you will end up with a long list of ideas. You will have some clichéd advice—put your best foot forward, step up, see the forest for the trees—but with a long list of ideas, you will be no closer to getting it!

That's because a long list of ideas is not the same as "getting it."

In fact, it is the opposite of getting it because you have no practical way of putting a long list of ideas to work. And with a long list of ideas you might confuse "getting it" as doing everything right.

Peter Drucker, the famed leadership expert, said, "Management is doing things right; leadership is doing the right things."

Getting It means that you do both—you do the right things, right!

Celebrated UCLA coach John Wooden says, "Don't mistake activity with achievement," and this step in *The System* works the same way. *Getting It* focuses on the right activity, which, like a chess Grandmaster, typically means that you have the greatest impact in the fewest number of moves.

Getting It, therefore, involves culling your long list of good ideas into a short list of the right ideas that have the greatest impact, enabling you to clearly focus on the activities that drive your career.

Imagine you are a senior associate in a law firm focused on making partner. A typical approach would be to keep doing what you are doing, while having all the "right" conversations. That might work for some, but it is a weak approach, and you will likely fail.

A better approach is to get incredibly strategic. On your external workstream, you might note you have built strong relationships, but to drive your career to the top, you must also meaningfully drive revenues. On your internal workstream, you realize you must raise your profile and you also must develop a thoughtful approach to getting the support of powerful decision-makers.

That's a strong approach. You are being thoughtful about doing the right activity that has the greatest impact. You have a much better shot, but relative to *Getting It,* this is still taking your chances in the pot! That's a gamble my clients never take.

Although that approach brings together some good ideas, *Getting It* is much more than stringing together good ideas. It's about developing your highly sophisticated, custom-built strategy for doing what you want.

THE INTELLIGENCE INSIDE THE SYSTEM

Getting It is the most important step in *The System for Doing What You Want!* While the other steps are rather mechanical, *Getting It* is the intelligence inside *The System.*

Personal development expert Brian Tracy says, "Life is a combination lock; your job is to find the right numbers, in the right order, so you can have anything you want." *Getting It* works the same way.

As you know *The System* is not about working harder. It's about working smarter, and *Getting It* is cracking the code of your career so that you have the right combination for getting what you want.

It's important to know that *Getting It* is not about taking actions or even planning to take actions. This happens when you develop and execute your plan in Steps 3 and 4. In *Getting It,* you develop your intelligence for building your plan. Here you are cunningly looking ahead on your roadmap, carefully developing your strategy by asking: *What must I do and who must I be for getting what I want?*

Going back to the example of the senior associate looking to make partner, you would plan your external and internal workstreams in detail. For instance, on your internal workstream, you are going far beyond raising your profile and getting support of key decision-makers, you are developing a sophisticated approach to winning by asking questions like:

- *WHO are my role models?*

- *WHAT are the models of success?*

- *HOW DO I develop my profile? My competitive advantage? My brand?*

Also, looking at the key decision-makers, you are thinking carefully about what is required to get their support. You are not just having the right conversations in the right way but developing a sophisticated approach to influencing each and every one of your decision-makers.

Putting it all together, like that chess Grandmaster, you think about all the pieces on the board and many moves ahead, bringing tremendous intelligence and developing your strategy for doing what you want.

★　　★　　★　　★　　★　　★

GETTING IT IS ABOUT YOU

You know those auto-biographies by famous leaders that people like to read? Well, I detest most of those books. Mostly written by ghost-writers, in glorious detail they tell you how great the author is, but how many of those books are written for making you great too?

You see, there's an enormous difference between knowing how others win and how you win. And there's an enormous difference between a system for doing what you want and *Your System*.

In *Getting It,* you are not just cracking the code of your career. You write your own code and determine your specific approach to winning. You go far beyond figuring out how *to* succeed; you develop your strategy for how *you* succeed.

★   ★   ★   ★   ★   ★

BUILDING YOUR STRATEGY IN
THREE STEPS

In the same way former professional diver Jason Statham has built a career playing a specific type of action hero, you must do the same.

Go deep into understanding how anyone wins in your career. Develop your self-knowledge of how you personally win, and match you and your career to build your strategy that is custom-built for you.

And while that might sound incredibly complex and sophisticated, we are making this easy by building up your strategy in three steps.

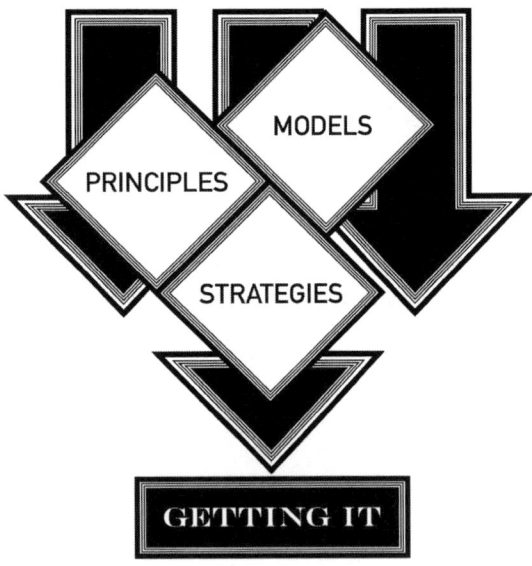

Applying the three steps of *Getting It,* we progress from the abstract idea of what leads to success in general to specifically defining your strategy for driving success in your career.

We begin at the highest level, the models of success that work in your career. Then we drop down a level to the principles before moving on to develop your strategy that is custom-built for you and your career.

Because that's what matters, right?

It's not about knowing how *to* succeed in your career, but how *you* succeed.

A SUGGESTION FOR YOU

I have a suggestion for getting the most value from *Getting It.*

Approach it from a clean slate—from the ground up. For a moment, set aside your current approach to success and open your mind to new ideas.

What matters most to *Getting It* is what matters most when you are fixing up that classic car: Take her paint back to metal, and re-work her from there. Remove her engine and break it down. Figure out what to replace and what to repair. Work on her inside, don't just touch up the upholstery, but see her for everything she can be.

In doing that, you are not working with where she is right now, you are breaking her all the way down and building her all the way back up. Don't ask: *How can I make her better?* Ask: *How can I make her the best she can be?*

The same is true in *Getting It.* It is not about incrementally improving your approach for winning in your career. From the ground up, from a clean slate, build yourself the absolute best strategy you can imagine for getting what you want.

If you can suspend your current beliefs and approach *Getting It* with an open mind, you will find as you reach the end, all of the ideas of *Getting It* will merge with your ideas, and you will develop for yourself your unique, incredibly powerful approach for getting what you want.

★   ★   ★   ★   ★   ★

A NOTE ON USING THESE IDEAS

In *Getting It,* I'm sharing with you a lot of different models, principles, and other ways of looking at your career. I am not suggesting that you need all of these ideas—none of the best people I modeled used any of these ideas—but rather I'm sharing with you concepts that enable you to custom-build your strategy for your career.

With my clients, we rely on these ideas to powerfully identify their best path for winning, and I suggest you use *Getting It* the same way.

So, remember, as you work your way through *Getting It*, the purpose is not for you to find a way to use all of these ideas, but for you to pick and choose the ideas that work best for you and your career.

CHAPTER TWELVE

THE MODELS

Munger defines Lollapalooza as the critical mass
obtained via a combination of concentration, curiosity,
perseverance, and self-criticism, applied through a prism
of multidisciplinary mental models.

—CHARLIE MUNGER, *POOR CHARLIE'S ALMANAC*

★   ★   ★   ★   ★   ★

A somewhat controversial figure in his industry, Bobby Kotick, CEO of Activision, has an incredibly deliberate strategy. And he is sticking to it.

Eschewing typical video game speak, Kotick consistently defines Activision's strategy as "narrow and deep" and "analyzable." He is not hunting for the next big thing. He is not shooting for the video game equivalent of Vanilla Ice. Instead, like Dr. Dre signing Eminem, Kotick is focused on franchises that "have the potential to be exploited every year on every platform with clear sequel potential and have the potential to become $100 million franchises."

Because of his strong financial focus, his strategy is less popular with video game enthusiasts, but it is a model that enabled him to build Activision from bankruptcy into an industry-leading $14 billion company. Whatever anyone might think of his strategy, it is a powerful model for success in his industry.

That's the point of the models. From a high level, know what models lead to success in your career. Next we cover two ways to model success in your career: Role Models and Modeling Roles.

ROLE MODELS

If you ask many people what leads to success in your career, they will likely list all those good ideas of what it means to "get it." I suggest a different approach. Rather than beginning with "what," begin with "who."

As Anthony Robbins says, "Success leaves clues."

Begin by creating a list of people who have succeeded in your career. Pay attention to the winners, then ask: *What works for them?*

Collect role models you can follow and your own path becomes clearer.

Rather than trying to go where there is no path and leave a trail, role models give you a path that has already been set.

The problem, then, is this: Because each person is a unique individual, rarely does anyone come across one role model who is a perfect fit.

But truth be told, that is good news because it leads us to a much better approach!

When I was in associate training at Goldman Sachs, I heard a piece of advice from a senior banker. The advice still resonates: "Rather than seeking out one great mentor for your career, instead seek out different mentors, each of whom embodies a quality you would like to develop."

But like most people who give great advice, she left me with no idea how to actually implement it. Fortunately, I have since learned the secret.

You create a model of a role model. By this, I mean: Take the best of your different role models, figure out what is right for you, and then build a composite role model—a "character," if you will—for who you are building yourself to be.

This method applies a sophisticated approach to modeling success that goes deeper than surface-level observations by breaking down how your role models do what they do.

MODELING ROLE MODELS

A presupposition of Neuro-linguistic Programming (NLP) is that if one person can do something, then every person can learn to do it. To teach excellence, NLP uses sophisticated tools that enable you to first model excellence and then break it down in a way for teaching others.

Consider this like the science behind how you are taught to ski. In the early days, you learned to ski by following an experienced skier, emulating his or her movements. But, as the sport evolved, to understand what led to good skiing, professors took black-and-white films of several skiers in the Alps. Studying them frame by frame, they sliced the flowing motion of skiing into "isolates," the smallest units of behavior. From there, they developed techniques to teach the skill of skiing by developing practices to cultivate the individual movements that, when put together, combine for good skiing.

Apply the same idea to modeling your role models. Observe what leads your role models to success, break down their successful behaviors, and then combine them into your composite role model. This works in three steps.

As we are working through the three steps, I want you to consider that the best way to identify what led another person to success is to ask him or her. But, in doing that, also remember that people quite often do not know what made them successful. So rather than having the experienced skiers try to break down what they do, scientists figured it out through observation—by paying careful attention to what leads to success and then breaking it down into the individual steps that anyone could learn to do.

Modeling your role models works the same way. You can learn a lot by asking them, but by observing them, you are more likely to best determine what they do and how you can do it too.

Here are the three steps.

STEP 1

WHAT?

The first step to modeling role models is to observe what they do. What makes them exceptional?

You want to go much deeper than, say, observing that a top advertising executive "has a feel for the market." Instead ask yourself things like: *What is it they do that gives them a feel for the market? Is it constant reading? And what? Newspapers and magazines? Online? Market research? Is it meeting with people? Discussing what? Is it from years of experience? From rigorous process and testing results?*

And, so on.

What about a top salesperson? You might observe that they are "phenomenal with people," but define your terms, break it down, and figure out: *What does "phenomenal" look like? Is it her interpersonal skills? Ability to earn trust? To step into another person's shoes? Really, what is it she does to be exceptional?*

A way to think about "What?" is to apply the two components of *The System*: process and skills.

1. PROCESS: Exceptional performance is a matter of process. Like Tiger Woods relies on a certain setup every time he steps up to the tee, determine what processes your role models use to do what they do? What are the processes that lead them to exceptional performance?

    For instance, does a great public speaker rehearse for weeks, as Steve Jobs used to do? Does he let someone else build the slides, or is he fully immersed in the ideas so that in the presentation he is delivering the ideas with the forcefulness of ownership?

2. SKILLS: Skiing is a skill built up using many different skills. Balance, agility, strength, and the like all build to the skill of skiing. The same is true for your role models. Ask yourself: *What skills do they most rely upon to be excellent?* For a paralegal it might be, say, their ability to filter through tons of information and determine what is of value. For a litigator, it might be exceptional skills of negotiation. What are the skills that drive success?

STEP 2

HOW?

"What?" is focused on physical behaviors. In "How?" you step deeper into understanding the mental strategies your role models use.

It is one thing to observe the skills and processes Warren Buffett applies, but to invest like Buffett, you must understand how he evaluates investments. In his case, it is easy. He tells you how he invests. And if you have the disposition to follow the ideology and strategies that Warren uses, you can invest like him too.

The same is true if you were to model his banker, Byron Trott, who has built a unique position with Buffett. To model his success, you would want to understand his specific strategies, which Buffett also tells you. As Buffett wrote in his 2008 investor letter, "Byron is the rare investment banker who puts himself in his client's shoes."

"How?" for Trott, then is this: He imagines himself in the shoes of his clients, seeing the world as they do, perhaps applying something similar to the performance tool of visualization.

In understanding the strategies your role models apply to winning, you can build a formidable set of ideas that enable you to build your own strategies for success.

STEP 3

WHY?

"Why?" is also easier to accomplish by questioning your role models. That doesn't necessarily mean that you interview them, but over time you can likely profile why they do what they do. "Why?" means to go deeper into their psyche to understand the thoughts that drive how and what they do.

Here are two filters to apply.

1. BELIEFS: What beliefs drive how your role model thinks about success? For instance, in the case of one of my CEO clients, he believes that as long as his business prospects are willing to think differently, they will eventually come around to his way of thinking. This is a belief that relates to his approach to selling, but look for personal beliefs too.

2. INTERNAL PROCESSING: If you can understand how your role model processes information internally, you will develop a strong understanding of his or her success. Few people can describe to you exactly what they do, but if you pay careful attention, you can discern it. A great presenter might not know they are using the performance tool of mental rehearsal, but in describing to you how they imagine a meeting playing out, they are giving you the clues.

So get inside the heads of your role models, and understand what internal processing drives their success. Do they talk themselves into top performance? Do they see a meeting playing out perfectly? Does an expert negotiator feel it when a negotiation is turning in his favor? Does a designer just have the conviction to trust her instincts? However it is that your role models process information in their minds, tease that out so that you can generalize and do it too.

PUTTING IT TOGETHER

In putting these ideas together, determine what aspects of your role models are idiosyncratic to them, and then assess how to combine your learnings in a way that works for you.

For instance, observing one role model, you might determine that he drives success by walking into a room and taking control (his "what?"). With his booming voice and commanding personality (his "how?"), it is easy for him to set the agenda. Yet you see that you have a different personality and style, so while his "what?" is of great value, you want a different "how?"

Looking at one of your other role models, you observe that she brings enormous value not through the force of her personality but from deep expertise, which is better suited to you.

When you think about your role models in this way, what you find is that you can build a composite role model that doesn't just take the best of how your role models win but also assesses what works best for you.

That's it for your role models. The next step is to model your role.

MODELING YOUR ROLE

Okay, here goes …

What you are going to see in this section might be quite different to any way you have ever thought about driving success in your career.

The reason this approach is incredibly powerful is because you are drilling deeper into the underlying structure of success, determining exactly what is valued in your career and role. By modeling your role, you focus on understanding the underlying structure of value.

What is powerful in getting to the underlying driver of success, what I call the models of success, is that once you understand your source of value, you can succeed in any and every role. I know that sounds vague, so let's go through the four models of success and allow it to become more clear.

I originally developed these models for a career on Wall Street, and although I have discussed them with many others in different careers, it's not to say that each of these models will be right for you. But as you work through these models they might trigger in you others that work best in your career.

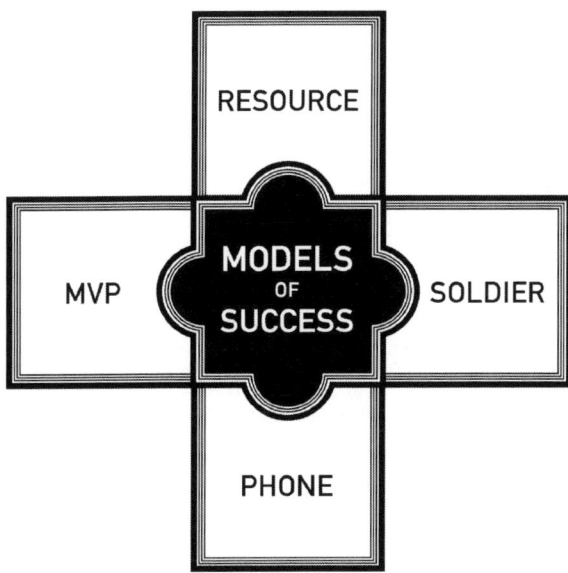

★ ★ ★ ★ ★ ★

THE RESOURCE MODEL

The resource model is a base model for thinking about your source of value. It is, in fact, the earliest model I developed for success in my career.

As a frustrated analyst filling in my timesheets, I grumbled things like, *I'm special. I'm not some damn resource measured according to capacity.*

But that's exactly what I was! To the staffer (who is responsible for allocating bankers to teams) and my teams, I was a substitutable resource—a commodity resource on a mostly commodity team. I resented that at first, but some years later as the staffer, I came to see just how right I had been.

As the staffer, I saw that no matter who you are (analyst, associate, vice president, division head, or even CEO), to someone else, you are just a resource.

You might not like that idea, but consider the most valuable person in your office. He or she must be an absolute rock star. People might say, "Man, if she ever left, we would be screwed."

But, now think back to the last rock star who left. Notice how quickly her seat was filled. That person might have been extremely valuable in your company, but in nearly every case I have come across, soon enough that person was replaced by another capable-enough person. In some cases they might not have been as good, in other cases they might have been better, but in almost all cases we are substitutable resources.

When you accept that you are a resource, you have the framework to understand and increase your source of value. Here's how.

You begin by asking: *In my job, what is valued?*

Are you like coal in that you are valued for the energy you burn, and your value is in working long hours? Or are you more like gold, where you drive value through having more value-add? Or perhaps your seat is more like a rare earth element, like Bucky Balls, where your value is now limitless.

It is important to note the models of success are judgment neutral. They do not say one is better or worse than the other. Instead, they give you a framework to assess what is valued so that you can provide more of this value (if you choose to do so). For instance, in most jobs at a junior level, you must see that you are valued as coal. While it might be nice to think of yourself as a source of value-add, first and foremost, you must see burning your energy and getting things done is your greatest source of value to your team.

The models of success also enable you to see that while success in any job is driven by many unique factors, the underlying driver of success can be exactly the same. For instance, for a partner in a consulting or law firm alike, being coal and working long hours is of little value relative to the unique perspectives and judgments they bring, which is ultimately their underlying source of value.

This resource model also shows you one way you can easily work fewer hours: Stop being coal and find ways to bring unique value. Like exchanging an ounce of gold for a truckload of coal, it's easy to work fewer hours when you are bringing more value.

★ ★ ★ ★ ★ ★

THE SOLDIER MODEL

The soldier model is a way to assess what is valued in your job and company.

You know in those war movies where they point to the guy at the end of the trench and signal that he is next to storm the hill? He tightens the strap on his helmet, checks his rifle and ammo, and says some parting words like, "See you in hell," before looking out from the trench, poking his head around and waiting for his moment. Then he scrambles out, beelining for cover, darting left to right, making big strides, and then—right when he has almost made it to cover…

BANG! He is shot.

He is the good soldier, and he sits on one extreme of the soldier model. In most careers the good soldier is the one who puts his head down and works hard and jumps on grenades for the team. He is of great value to the company, but he is also the easiest to underpay, overlook, and sacrifice when you need to make cuts.

At the other extreme is the mercenary. She is a rōnin, looking out for herself at every turn. Working hard for the team, she always has one foot out the door. It can pay to be a mercenary. That type of confidence and credible threat can be highly valued, but being a mercenary has its limitations, especially if you work for a company that favors a team culture.

With the good soldier and mercenary as the bookends, there are other models in between. For instance, some people are lieutenants. They do what they are asked but they do it in their own way and take on leadership positions. Others are generals, valued as leaders.

The key to using the soldier model is observing what is valued in your company and in your role. Take a look around and notice how playing different roles works for others around you. And notice what types of patterns are at work in your company. You might see many rely on one soldier-type or another, or that certain combinations of models of success go together.

One of the most successful bankers I have ever met is a classic good soldier. He bleeds for the firm. He will never leave, and the firm knows it. He does what is asked: storms every hill, puts his head down and works hard. While that is a recipe to be shot, it works for him because he is also palladium. He is exceptional. In a role of great value, he has an incredibly unique skill set. This is a combination that works well for the good soldier.

In modeling your role, you might also observe, like Stallone and Schwarzenegger, over the course of your career, it pays to play different soldier-types at different points in time. And what matters is knowing how to use different roles as underlying drivers of value.

THE PHONE MODEL

The phone model is about how your choices embed value in your role.

Among other things, the phone model answers the question of whether you are best to specialize because it gives you a better way of framing success according to sources of value. It's called the phone model because, like a phone, your value in your career is either fixed or mobile.

The mobile model is one of a generalist, a chameleon who takes on different roles and builds her value through flexibility. She is perceived to be a good athlete, someone you want on your team, who can adapt and be successful in different roles. In contrast, the fixed model is one of a specialist, whose model of success is like a building with a deep and strong foundation, such as a well-entrenched salesperson whose value is deep, long-standing relationships.

The power of the phone model is that it enables you to get beyond the surface-level drivers of success to the underlying structure of success. It is not a question of whether you should be a specialist or generalist; it is understanding how each role connotes different value.

Consider a consultant who is a generalist relative to one who specializes by sector. While either one of them might be more or less successful, what matters is the way in which they drive success. Whereas the generalist will seek to drive value by sharing insights gathered across different industries, a specialist will seek to bring value through a deep understanding of his or her specialty. That doesn't mean that, as a specialist, you cannot also be more mobile, but when you understand the source of your value is remaining fixed, you can better assess the risk to your career in becoming more mobile. Playing with the phone model, you see there are many variations on these ideas.

However you choose, what matters most to deploying the phone model is knowing your source of value today and in the future and building your career by making the right call.

★   ★   ★   ★   ★   ★

THE MVP MODEL

The MVP model is a way to conceptualize the different sources of value you bring to each of your teams (where applicable) and your company.

Think of it like a basketball team. There are five distinct positions on the court and each player has a unique value he brings to the team. For instance, one player's source of value might be his ability to score big in any one game while another might be valued for his consistency. In this way the MVP model enables you to assess what roles are valued on your team and which ones are right for you to fill.

For instance, consider a model for a Hollywood production company. Some producers might be like a steady performer focused on creating a consistent stream of low-budget productions, while others might be more like a three-point specialist focused on producing big budget hits. Both are distinctly different but valuable roles.

However you think of it, the MVP model gives you a way of conceptualizing different roles and sources of value, enabling you to establish your value in different ways inside your company, depending on what's required and valued.

EXERCISE

ROLE MODELS AND MODELING ROLES

Now that we have worked through the models, take some time to go back and review what we have covered.

As you read back through the chapter, I suggest you create a summary table plotting your role models against the models of success. You might also identify other models of success that you believe are applicable to you in your career.

	RESOURCE	SOLDIER	PHONE	MVP
MODEL 1				
MODEL 2				
MODEL 3				
MODEL 4				
MODEL 5				

So look around you and at your different role models, and ask yourself: *What are their models of success? What roles do they play to drive value?*

Notice any trends that jump out at you and also what your table suggests about building your composite role model—your "character."

Like Bobby Kotick of Activision, in understanding the underlying drivers of success, you are well on your way to developing your formula for driving deep value in your career.

CHAPTER THIRTEEN

THE PRINCIPLES

Principles are concepts that can be applied over and over again in similar circumstances as distinct from narrow answers to specific questions.

— RAY DALIO, *PRINCIPLES*

★　★　★　★　★　★

A common theme in my work is distilling enormous amounts of information down to the most important ideas. Those ideas are the principles. Like my Two Secrets for Doing What You Want, principles are the dominant ideas—the driver of all other ideas. In understanding the principles, you understand what drives all other ideas.

Ralph Waldo Emerson said, "As to methods, there may be a million and then some, but principles are few. The man who grasps principles can successfully select his own methods."

Once you understand the principles of *Getting It,* rather than having to figure out the next right idea, you have the ideas that drive all the right ideas.

For example, consider the skill of time management. There's an infinite list of good productivity tips: Shut down your email, stop web surfing, delegate, schedule meetings and calls. These are all good ideas, but they are merely low-level ideas that represent a much more powerful principle.

And that is my second principle of time management: Shift your time to its highest-value use. In shifting your time to its highest-value use, you no longer think about: *Shut down my email and stop web surfing.*

Instead, you are simply asking: *What is the highest-value use of my time?* And then you put your time there!

One of Bruce Lee's famous principles is: Be like water. Move and strike with fluidity. Never think about punches and kicks and movement. Instead, fight with the ease from which every movement and strike simply flows.

Similarly, applying the principles of *Getting It*, you are focused on what truly matters: putting to work the principles and allowing them to trickle down like a well-functioning economy into the lower-value ideas.

THE PRINCIPLES WORK

In *The Code Book*, Simon Singh reveals one of the earliest approaches to cracking ciphers. To overcome having to run the billions of possible combinations, cipher-breakers developed a novel approach called frequency analysis.

They analyzed the common frequency of letters used in the language of the code. For instance, in the English language, the letter "e" is the most commonly used letter, appearing with a frequency of around twelve percent. Then, substituting the commonly occurring letters with the corresponding appearance of letters in the cipher, they quickly cracked the code.

The principles of *Getting It* were derived much the same way. By modeling success over many years, I focused on cracking the code in my career. Paying careful attention to what led others to success, I was modeling the high frequency factors that drive success. Then, over time, I generalized these ideas into the principles.

★   ★   ★   ★   ★   ★

MASTERY IN FIVE PRINCIPLES

You get to principles by reverse engineering.

You begin learning most topics by focusing on an increasing amount of small detail, the tactics, and the techniques. For instance, when you learned to ride a bike, you were first introduced to the handlebars for steering and to the pedals for speed, the brakes for stopping, and given instructions on balancing the bike.

In the beginning, that's all you thought about. But having mastered the basics, you come to learn that the tactics and techniques you learned were based on more powerful principles. In the case of riding a bike, you learned the principle of motion when you learned about balance and steering.

As children, of course, we were unable to conceptualize a principle first, but now that we are adults, we can start with the principles and build the small details on top of a powerful foundation.

That's powerful, and so too is this.

Not only did my years of research lead me to conclude the importance of principles, I also came to believe that you can master any subject by understanding the five principles that drive success.

That's right. You can master any topic by mastering just five principles.

Now, before we get to the five principles of *Getting It*, let's begin with the sixth principle!

★ ★ ★ ★ ★ ★

THE SIXTH PRINCIPLE

I know. I just got done telling you that there are five principles. But I'm starting with the sixth principle because it is a meta-principle.

In the same way that "learning" is a meta-principle (because knowing how to learn you can learn all things), the sixth principle similarly drives the five principles of *Getting It*. If all you did is master this one meta-principle, you will master all the other principles—as well as your career!

The sixth principle is the most important lesson I learned in my career and drives all of my work.

This is the idea that drives all of your goals: Getting paid, promoted, working fewer hours, creating more career options, and ultimately transforming your career and creating the life you truly want.

So, what is it? What idea can possibly be so powerful that it's all you need for getting what you want?

VALUE! The sixth principle is Value!

Einstein said, "Try not to become a man of success, but rather try to become a man of value."

The sixth principle sees your career the same way. Rather than focus on success, focus on the source of all success—creating value.

How do you get paid? By driving more value.

Promoted? By being of greater value.

Work less hours? Create more value.

Create more career options? Be of greater value.

Value drives success in everything you do. So if you don't remember everything else, remember value.

Value, value, value, value, value, value, value, value, value, value, value, value, value, value, value, value, value, value, value.

Value.

Whatever you want in your career is only possible so long as you can justify what you want in the value you are creating.

Think about it this way: If you are sitting in the corner office and someone walked in wanting to get paid more, wouldn't you want them to have contributed more of what you value? Is that more client relationships? Is that more P&L? Is it better ideas? Is it an alternate job offer as leverage? It might be all or any number of these things, but to be sure, to give more money to them, you would want them to have delivered you more value.

What's powerful in understanding the sixth principle is that it is the dominant idea driving all other ideas.

When you understand the dominant power of value, you see that every single way of thinking about your career becomes clear through the lens of value. And the same is true with the five principles. Seen through the lens of value, each of the five principles is enormously magnified.

★　★　★　★　★　★

THE FIVE PRINCIPLES OF *GETTING IT*

As we discussed, I arrived at the five principles by taking all other ideas and aggregating, generalizing, and refining those ideas to determine what I consider the dominant ideas for getting what you want in your career.

Although I have spent years discussing these principles with people in different industries and observed they apply well across different careers, only you can know if they are right for you in your career. Even if these principles are not right for you, they will likely help you hone in on those that are.

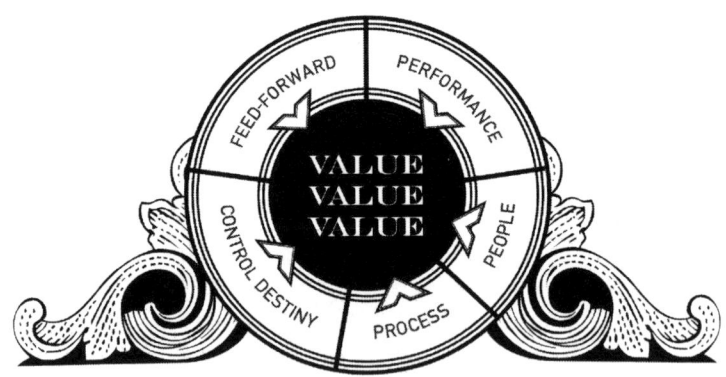

PERFORMANCE

First and foremost, *Getting It* means performance.

Whatever soft, touchy-feely topics you hear from me, this first principle comes down to cold, hard performance.

Performance is the number-one principle because it's what matters most to getting what you want. Without performance, you will fail. Yet, with performance, everything is possible. Getting paid more, getting promoted faster, whatever it is: Creating more options is easy when you are delivering crushing performance.

Performance means going far beyond lists of low-level ideas about being more effective. It means truly knowing which performance factors drive success in your career.

For instance, in your career you will hear tons of criteria used to measure performance. But performance means knowing what is truly valued and rewarded. Think of the times when someone says that you should be more of a culture carrier and get more involved in recruiting, or that taking on administrative tasks inside your company will increase your profile and get you access to decision-makers.

You should ignore them and their terrible advice. As a top officer at a large bank recently said to my client, "No one makes partner running recruiting."

Beyond knowing which performance factors are valued in your company, performance means actually being able to—well, perform. This requires a good dose of honesty about your current performance and, where required, the commitment to improving your performance.

Think about that now. Ask yourself: *What does it mean to be performing? Who am I performing for? What standards do they have for me, and what matters to getting there?*

If you can do that, you are already most of the way to getting what you want.

<hr />

PRINCIPLE 2

PEOPLE

Nearly every professional career is a people business, right?

How many times have you heard that? But, how many people in your "people business" do you know who have trained to be exceptional with people? And I'm not talking reading some book on leadership or attending a two-day skills program. I'm talking about becoming masterful with people. *Getting It* is about getting good, if not truly exceptional, with people.

Working well with people is paramount to success in nearly every facet of a professional career. Externally, whether you are in consulting, law, architecture, and most other industries, being a people person is how you generate revenues. Internally, this is crucial to getting paid and promoted. Literally, in most professional jobs nearly everything you do happens with people.

So if you want to get good at everything in your career, then get better than good with people.

Doing that first requires some self-evaluation. Many people operate at a fraction of their potential by perceiving that they are already good communicators. They therefore fail to exceptionally train their skills.

How many people in your people business believe they have above-average communication skills? I bet you can name a good number.

But how many have trained their skills? What have they done to get good with people? Have they read any books? Taken any courses?

Many who perceive themselves to be "naturals" are unconsciously incompetent. They fail to know how bad they are, let alone how exceptional they could be with a small amount of effort.

The truth is, people set a low bar for themselves. While this is sad, it's also great news for you because by studying and becoming exceptional with people, you can easily run circles around "naturals."

Start by reading and, more importantly, practicing the ideas of *How To Win Friends and Influence People* by Dale Carnegie, *Influence* by Robert Cialdini, and *What Every BODY is Saying* by Joe Navarro.

Then take it all the way and learn NLP and conversational hypnosis. You will be able to do things other people don't know people do!

PRINCIPLE 3

PROCESS

Carefully observe, and you will see that everything in your life happens through process—from the way you brush your teeth to the way you commute to work.

Most jobs are the same. It requires managing process.

Consider my friend who is an executive chef managing a high-end restaurant. Like a car rolling its way down a production line, meals are prepared in a series of process steps that run from the beginning to a finished product at the end. The same is true as it relates to my former client who is responsible for managing teams of engineers developing games. Building games, as with most things in life, happens through a well-executed process.

Processes are not solely for defining tasks. Managing people, including yourself, is a process. And so too is managing the process of your career. Internally, externally, macro, and micro, throughout this guide, you are developing numerous processes for putting to work in your career.

Implied in this principle is that to get what you want, you must become excellent at managing process. That means that you look at your job in the same way a mechanical engineer looks at a manufacturing process, focusing on sequence, steps, and work-flow, continuously enhancing efficiency, effectiveness, and quality.

PRINCIPLE 4

CONTROL DESTINY

A few years back I had a conversation with an investment banking managing director. He was a company man on his way from good soldier to general.

Having done well for more than a decade, and doing many of the right things, he had quickly ascended. By all accounts, he was on the partner track. You would have thought he would have a long and prosperous career. Until one day that changed.

His business slowed down.

His partner track ended.

He was laid-off.

When we spoke, he was beside himself. He had done all the right things. He had taken the right jobs. He had been told that he was on the partner track. He was more than a resource that could be discarded if the business slowed down, right?

Wrong.

It was obvious to me where he failed. If you think that by doing what is asked, you will keep ascending, think again! You keep ascending by knowing what is valued and by controlling your destiny.

As Jack Welch said, "Control your own destiny or someone else will."

The opposite of keeping your head down and working hard, controlling your destiny means that you focus on where you are headed, and then you drive your career there.

The same is true when it comes to getting paid and promoted. Think about it this way: Most people trying to get promoted hang back. They do some things right. They have some conversations. But how many take control of the process of promotion? How many have a detailed plan and take control of making it happen?

PRINCIPLE 5

FEED-FORWARD

Feed-forward is my favorite principle because it's a little sneaky. And we all like to be a little bit sneaky.

Whereas the first four principles relate to how you are getting your job done, feed-forward relates to something slightly different—to how others know you are getting your job done. Whereas the other principles are about creating value in your career, feed-forward is about broadcasting the value you create.

Here's the thing: You can keep your head down, work hard, and hope someone notices and reflects it in your feedback. Or you can take charge of driving the perception of you.

Feed-forward is about managing the perception of your performance and your performance reviews. It's the extreme of controlling your destiny in that rather than letting your destiny be driven by your feedback, you flip the script and feed-forward information and drive your own destiny.

Think of it this way: In taking a driving test, you know what you must do. When getting your motorcycle license, you must do a slow circle with little throttle. In a car, you must parallel park. In preparing for your test, then, you practice over and over, ensuring that you easily pass the test.

Think of the way you are assessed the same way. You never want your feedback to say you have failed. Instead, in knowing what is on the test, feed-forward your success throughout the year.

Rather than waiting for year-end feedback, informally collect feedback throughout the year, then correct your performance, and feed-forward the ideas you want reflected about you.

For instance, consider a senior consultant who is perceived to be deficient at building client relationships. While fixing this deficiency matters, what matters more to his success is that others know he is fixing it.

While he is working on fixing this deficiency, he can make comments and send e-mails like, "I'm focused on improving my skills to build client relationships, and I would appreciate your ideas."

In the heartbeat his boss takes to write his review, what do you guess she will scribe? Perhaps something like: *He has really stepped it up with clients.*

Don't get me wrong: Feedback is important to your development because it helps you get better and better, and I encourage you to seek as much feedback as possible. Yet, I also suggest collecting feedback only in ways that enable you to feed-forward your success.

The truth is: Nothing matters more to your success than how you are perceived.

The market for your success is highly inefficient, and if you are relying on others to discover your success and promote you, you will be waiting a long time.

ALL OR NONE?

A common question I get is: *What matters more, to be proficient at all of the principles or become exceptional at just one?*

The answer is this: What matters is that you are materially deficient at none. Let me give you an example.

In 1991, when a young unknown Brazilian jiu-jitsu champ Royce Gracie walked into the cage of the bare-knuckled UFC, he was able to quickly destroy every one of his opponents by taking them down and dismantling their joints on the ground.

In schooling other top fighters, catching them in and off guard, Gracie fundamentally changed the direction of MMA, and other fighters soon realized something: While you don't need to become a master of BJJ, successfully competing requires at the least not being deficient on the ground.

So like MMA, it's not crucial that you are exceptional at all of the principles, but you must at least be proficient at each of them.

Once you've got all the principles down, like a top fighter, you can master and exploit the ones that best drive success for you in your career.

GOING DEEPER

As Groucho Marx said, "Those are my principles, and if you don't like them…well, I have others."

This book covers the principles at a high level. I'm writing a separate book that will go much deeper, showing you how to become a master at these principles and how to add sub-principles to increase the rate at which you get what you want.

—— **EXERCISE** ——

HOW DO YOU STACK UP?

Now that you are familiar with the principles, I suggest working back through this section and assessing your current grasp of the principles.

You might want to create a summary table measuring yourself against the five principles and also identifying next steps for your development.

You might also identify some of your own principles, which you consider to be right for you and your career.

	ASSESSMENT	DEVELOPMENT
1. PERFORMANCE		
2. PEOPLE		
3. PROCESS		
4. CONTROL DESTINY		
5. FEED-FORWARD		
6. VALUE, VALUE, VALUE		

CHAPTER FOURTEEN

THE STRATEGIES

Absorb what is useful, reject what is useless, add what is specifically your own.

— BRUCE LEE

★　　★　　★　　★　　★　　★

If you have ever had a suit made on Savile Row, you understand the value of an exceptional custom tailor.

You find yourself immersed in the process of having a custom suit fitted to you. You walk through a room full of the finest fabrics, learning the differences and figuring out what works best for your frame. From there, you move to design—turning through pages of designs, choosing the style, colors, and combinations that are right for you.

Once you are done making choices, the work begins. You now have all the right inputs for your custom-fitted suit, but that's not where an expert tailor shines. That's not why you are here.

The real magic happens next when you have that suit custom-fitted to you.

The same is true with *Getting It*. In the first two steps, we covered an abundance of ideas for doing what you want in your career. And while we might have already gone far beyond any career advice you've ever seen, it is the next step—the strategies—where the magic is done.

While the models and the principles are powerful universal ideas that work in any career at every level, in tailoring these ideas specifically for you, they become devastatingly potent. That's because *Getting It* is not about identifying what works well for others but what works specifically for you.

Getting It is about building your custom-tailored strategy for doing what you want. There is no universal definition of *Getting It*. There is only your unique definition of *Getting It* that is custom-fitted for you.

$$\star \quad \star \quad \star \quad \star \quad \star \quad \star$$

MATCHING TO YOU

In pairing the universal ideas with your self-knowledge, you create an unstoppable formula for success. And while this might sound like a revolutionary approach, in fact, I'm just sharing a sophisticated way of doing what some of the most successful people I've modelled already do.

For instance, when one of my former bosses joined Goldman Sachs as a vice president, he decided to interview thirty-five of the firm's top bankers to learn the secrets to their success. While he developed a good list of ideas from these interviews, what surprised him was that the predominate advice had little to do with the nuances of being a good banker. It didn't relate to better serving clients or hidden wisdom on winning business. In fact, it had nothing to do with clients or business.

Instead, it was to drive success through self-knowledge.

Similarly, in his book *What You're Really Meant To Do,* former vice chairman of Goldman Sachs and professor at Harvard Business School, Rob Kaplan discusses a similar theme, citing what he learned over decades in business and emphasizing the importance of knowing who you are and playing to your strengths.

That is precisely what we will do in the strategies—bridge together the best ideas for what leads to success in every career (the models and the principles) with your self-knowledge to develop your custom-tailored strategy for your career.

We do this in three steps.

1. AGGREGATE THE MODELS and the principles and determine the strategies that lead to success.

2. MIX IN self-knowledge.

3. DETERMINE your strategy for succeeding in your career.

THE STRATEGIES

The strategies are a summary of the first two steps. Here we lay out your career in accordance with the models and the principles, identifying the strategies that lead to success.

As an example, I'm sharing the strategies I developed in assessing my career as an investor at the Carlyle Group.

CATEGORY	COMMENT
ROLE MODELS	HOWARD MARKS, SETH KLARMAN
MODELS OF SUCCESS	
1. RESOURCE MODEL	COAL IRRELEVANT. VALUE IS UNCOVERING DIAMONDS IN THE ROUGH.
2. SOLDIER MODEL	MUST BE A GENERAL. HAVE TO LEAD. HAVE A VIEW. DRIVE VALUE.
3. PHONE MODEL	MUST BE MOBILE. ACROSS INDUSTRIES AND CAPITAL STRUCTURE.
4. MVP	STEADY, PLUS HOME RUN POTENTIAL. PUBLIC OR PRIVATE EXPERTISE.
THE PRINCIPLES	
1. PERFORMANCE	INVESTMENT PERFORMANCE IS PERFORMANCE.
2. PEOPLE	LESS INTERNAL. INFORMATION EDGE AND DRIVING VALUE IN CONTROL.
3. PROCESS	INVESTMENT PROCESS IS EVERYTHING.
4. CONTROL DESTINY	SPEND TIME WHERE I DRIVE FUND VALUE.
5. FEED-FORWARD	LESS RELEVANT. PERCEPTION YOU ARE GETTING IT.

At the top of the table, you see two role models: Seth Klarman and Howard Marks. For developing my skills as an investor, I read hundreds of papers and books, and I developed strong affinity with the value school of investing. As role models I used Klarman and Marks, not just because they are the best in the business, but also because they publish valuable ideas, which made it easy to model their approaches and apply their ideas.

Next are the models of success. You can see what I perceived as value-drivers at Carlyle. Remember that the strategies don't relate generally to any career but are specific to your job and firm, so these are not generic to investing, but specific to my job at Carlyle.

Unlike my jobs at Goldman Sachs, the principles at Carlyle were more straightforward and oriented to uncovering value and driving performance through exceptional investment process. Principle 2 (People) was more important on private market transactions, with a different bent to banking and almost non-existent on driving success inside my group. All this together, you see a simple summary of the strategies that I perceived led to success at Carlyle.

And while this is a simple summary, it's merely a starting point. From here it is easy to continue building these ideas.

For instance, beyond this table, there are two factors that drove all the strategies for success at Carlyle. The first factor is the underlying three-step process I developed for driving all investment success—sourcing, process, and execution—which requires developing expertise for each.

The second factor was recognizing the two tracks for success: investing in public securities and investing in private companies. Akin to a business-focused law firm where you can choose a career focused on securities offerings or mergers & acquisitions, at Carlyle I could choose to build expertise in either public or private investing. While it's important to be good at both, I knew I had to pair the strategies with my self-knowledge to develop my strategy for success and build true competitive advantage as an investor.

With this simple table, we take all the complexity of your career and develop a way to think about the strategies that drive success. From here, you can pick and choose and, most importantly, begin matching these ideas with your self-knowledge to develop your custom-tailored strategy.

★　★　★　★　★　★

DEVELOPING YOUR SELF-KNOWLEDGE

In 1100 BC, two words were inscribed in stone on the oldest and most influential religious sanctuary in ancient Greece, the temple in Delphi. This was one of the birthplaces of modern knowledge, and into the wall of the temple, these were the two words carved: Know Thyself.

While self-knowledge is a worthwhile pursuit one should spend a lifetime cultivating, for our purpose, let's draw a narrow career definition of "Know Thyself." For us, this means focusing on three categories of self-knowledge.

YOUR LIKES

By far, the most important aspect to success is your desire and willingness to do what it takes. And by far the most assured way of you doing what it takes is liking what you do.

Identify the aspects of your career you truly enjoy. Is it being with people? Getting things done? Thinking strategically? What's exciting and energizing?

Now, thinking about the strategies you identified, what roles do you most enjoy? How could you most enjoy your work by building your career around those roles?

Think about the choices I outlined for my career at Carlyle. Public and private market investing are extremely different day-to-day jobs.

By choosing the roles you like, you are more willing to lean in and do what it takes to win. How does that relate in your career? What choices orient your job more to your likes?

YOUR STRENGTHS

A common theme in the literature of success is that rather than focusing on improving your weaknesses, position yourself to capitalize on your strengths. I agree!

There are two steps to this. The first is: Know your strengths. The second is: Work with them.

You probably have a good sense for your strengths, but if you don't, there are obvious ways to figure it out. You might look back and see where your strengths have enabled you to excel. You might ask others and reflect on reviews and feedback to see how other people define your strengths and deficiencies. While it's not always easy to be honest, the more honest you can be, the better your strategy.

From there, it's a matter of figuring out how you orient your career to play to your strengths. Can you direct your current job? Or will you be better off making a slight or major course correction, over time orienting your career to play to your strengths? Whatever it might be, think about how you can win by playing to your strengths.

KNOW YOU!

If you have ever taken a personality test such as Myers-Briggs, you have a good idea for where you fit in the spectrum of personality types. But you never need to have taken such a test to have a good sense for who you are. Think about these three categories, and in particular, think about them with reference to how you best align yourself to win.

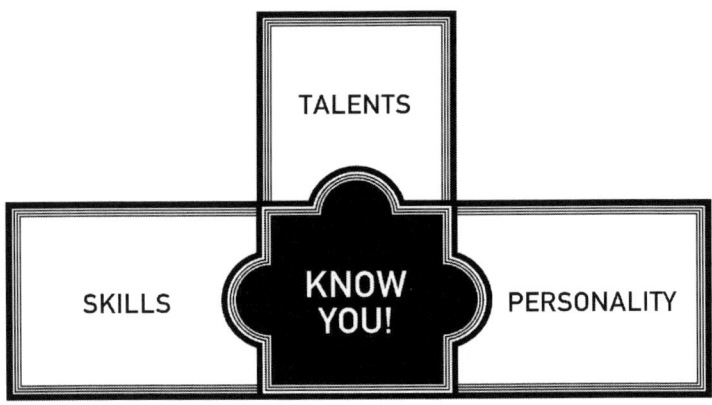

What are your talents? What comes naturally to you? Like someone who can easily grasp a page of numbers or who can walk into a room and speak with anyone, which of your talents drive your success?

What are your skills? And think not only about the obvious skills, but also the skills behind the skills? Which of your skills enable you to drive massive value?

How do you describe your personality? Are you serious? Fun? Cool? Quiet and reserved? A difficult jerk? What describes you, and how might someone else describe you?

As businessman and former Mayor of New York Michael Bloomberg put it: "Stubborn isn't a word I would use to describe myself. Pigheaded is more appropriate."

Remember to be honest, even if it's not particularly positive by other people's standards. A senior executive recently told me he was not a team player. While many people would say that sheepishly, he wasn't sheepish about this quality. He was just factual. And that type of self-knowledge enabled him to be incredibly successful.

YOUR STRATEGY

Having covered the strategies and self-knowledge, I'm sure you can see what comes next. That's right, we're slotting the pieces together creating your strategy.

While I wish there was a neat way to graphically represent this idea of developing a framework for matching you and your career, the truth is this: It's more like you are stirring these ideas in a pot and cooking up your strategy.

Consider the example of my career at Carlyle. I determined the best strategy was building expertise at either public or private investing. I then developed my career through focusing on the three steps in the process of investing: sourcing, process, and execution.

Having identified these two paths, I began matching my self-knowledge, considering my likes, strengths, and who I am relative to the public or private market specialties. While public and private investing are similar in many ways, they are in fact extremely different jobs. They have a different orientation, and they appeal to different types of people. So when I broke down the investment process into sourcing, process, and execution, I saw that the day-to-day investment processes suit a different personality and set of skills.

Whatever the circumstances of your career, you see combining the strategies with self-knowledge leads to particularly enlightening ideas on developing your strategy.

So, having put all these ideas into the mixing pot, you can build your strategy for your career.

While we are simply touching on these ideas, you might spend weeks or even months bringing together all the ideas of *Getting It* in building your strategy that's custom-tailored for you.

Now before we finish *Getting It,* let's go one enormous step further.

*　　*　　*　　*　　*　　*

1 PLUS 1 EQUALS 11

In the spirit of taking you as far as you want to go, we are going to take you one massive leap further. Going beyond your strategy, we will focus on building you into a player of such great value that anything is possible.

We do that by thinking about your strategy for building unique value—your competitive advantage.

Jack Welch says, "if you don't have a competitive advantage, don't compete."

You want the same to be true for you. You want your strategy to do more than help you win. You want to build your competitive advantage, which gives you a sustainable advantage for winning.

And then, on top of your competitive advantage, you want to build something even more powerful too. Let me give a definition by way of example.

One of my clients is an investment banking partner focused on developing his edge. In our work, we have defined his strategy for success. We have built for him processes and skills and determined how he plays to his competitive advantage.

We have also gone another massive leap further. He does not want to walk into a room, do his pitch, and hope he wins. He does not want to call on a client for years hoping to build a relationship. He wants to be a banker who has a brand that brings deals and clients to him.

Think about that for a moment. Rather than having to compete the way everyone else does, how would it be if you built yourself into a brand that brings business to you? While it might not sound realistic, that's how it works for the most successful people.

You don't have to work on Wall Street to have heard of one of the wealthiest men on the planet, Warren Buffett. Not only is he perhaps the greatest investor of all time, Warren has built a personal brand that gives him exclusive access to investments on his terms.

Or consider famous attorney Gloria Allred. In a legal career that has spanned over three decades she has built for herself a powerful brand that brings certain-types of high profile cases to her.

Similarly, look at Silicon Valley and you see any number of venture capitalists who have built superstar brands that bring companies to them, such as Marc Andreessen and Ben Horowitz.

I bet the same is true in your profession. Just think for a moment about the most prominent professionals in your industry. They are not only exceptional at what they do, but they have built a brand that draws business to them.

So, think about that. If others have built powerful brands, why can't you? With the steps we have outlined, and your expert understanding of what drives value in your career, what's stopping you putting it all together and building for yourself a powerful brand?

Nothing. Now you have all of the pieces for *Getting It*, you have the tools you need to build your strategy and brand for driving your career anywhere you want to go.

With all those answers, now all you need is a plan for making it happen. So, how do you that? How do you go from knowing how you win to taking the actions to get what you want?

You do that the same way you'd tackle any complex task. You *plan*.

CHAPTER FIFTEEN

PLAN IT

A goal without a plan is just a wish.

— ANTOINE DE SAINT-EXUPÉRY

★　★　★　★　★　★

Imagine that you pull into the construction site of the dream home you are building. You say good day to the foreman and tell him you are just stopping by to see how things are going.

To your left you see a messy pile of wood looking like enormous matchsticks strewn on the ground. To your right, a crew of workers is busily pouring concrete into what appears to be a foundation for your home. Ahead of you, a frame appears to be going up. But it looks nothing like the blueprint of your dream home.

Confused, you turn to the foreman.

"This looks nothing like the plan. What's going on?"

As if shocked by your question, the foreman responds with, "What plan? We were told to just get building."

You would never—never!—build your dream home that way, yet this is how most of us build our careers. You might spend months, even years, planning and building a home, yet when it comes to our careers, which is where we spend most the days of our lives, few of us spend even hours developing a plan. Instead, with grand ambition, we ferociously get building.

Like a lengthy business plan, career planning can seem onerous, if we know how to do it at all. But just like lengthy business plans are mostly useless, so too is a detailed career plan.

What you do need is a plan that enables you keep driving your career. Done right, it takes little time. And, more importantly, planning saves you time by enabling you to direct your time in a way that is impactful.

And contrary to popular belief, your career is *not* too complex to plan any more than a home is too complex to plan. In fact, it is absurd to think that a complex career mitigates the need for a plan. It is because your career is complex that you need a plan!

What you need is a simple and efficient approach to planning that is built for the complexity of your career. That's *The Plan*.

THE PLAN

We are typically taught to think of the planning and execution phases as separate steps: First you draw up a plan, then you execute.

While that approach works well for building your house—where inputs and outputs are fixed and determinable—there's little value to this approach in a dynamic and uncertain career. After all, your plan might be outdated as soon as it is drawn up!

The Plan takes this into account and works differently.

Rather than building a rigid plan, which you polish to perfection before you begin executing, *The Plan* is an iterative process of continuous planning and executing. Planning and execution are not separate steps; instead, they form a dynamic and integrated process.

Winston Churchill said, "However beautiful the strategy, you should occasionally look at the results."

The Plan works the same way by giving you a process for continuously planning, executing, and testing your results, working and re-working your plan over and over as you get what you want.

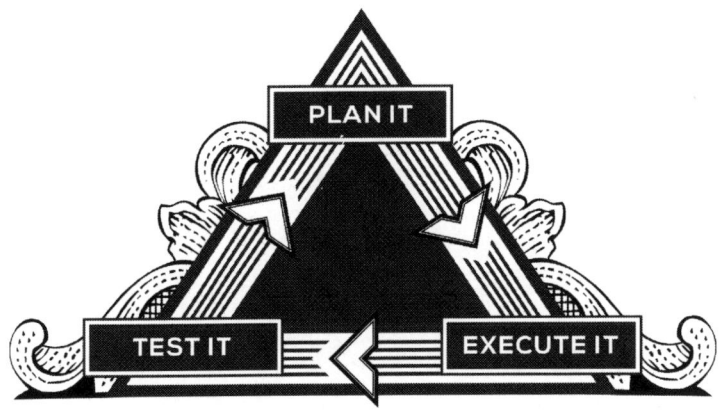

So, although *Plan It* and *Execute It* are separate steps in *The System for Doing What You Want!*, think of your plan as fluid, constantly in flow, planning and executing over time.

For example, imagine you are a vice president of business development with the goal of running your company. You begin executing your plan today, and as you keep taking steps and making progress moving toward your goal, you keep updating your plan. You keep planning new ways to execute, which you implement immediately, working and re-working all the way to running your company.

Doing this not only enables you to easily keep driving your career, it also makes you highly adaptable to change. As Mike Tyson said, "Everyone has a plan till they get punched in the mouth."

Like a fighter is constantly testing and adapting his fight plan, you too are constantly adapting your plan for whatever your career throws at you.

PLAN IT

A PLAN IS ESSENTIAL

Most of us just like to get on with things, don't we? Yet planning is essential. Through thoughtful and deliberate action, you typically get your best results. And although your career is a complex process with a well-developed plan, even the most complex process can be broken down into simple and logical steps.

For instance, consider another incredibly complex process—an education.

You spend the better part of the first two decades of your life in school. From learning your ABCs all the way through your SATs you develop an enormous amount of knowledge.

Looking back on decades of learning you see that knowledge was built up for you in a methodical way that enabled you to keep progressing year after year.

Can you imagine how you would learn if all that knowledge was simply thrown at you in one year? Instead it is planned out and fed to you one piece at a time.

Now think about your career. How much more complex is it? How much more choice do you have? How much more is required for you to figure out along the way? Does it not seem ludicrous to just keep working away without a plan?

As Benjamin Franklin said, "By failing to prepare, you are preparing to fail."

DEVELOPING YOUR PLAN

In the definitive book on taking action, *Getting Things Done*, David Allen poses the question: "How much planning do you really need to do?"

He goes on to write, "The simple answer is, as much as you need to get the project off your mind."

That's how I suggest approaching *Plan It.* Your plan is not designed to be a treatise on your career. It is merely the tool you need to keep powerfully driving your career.

When it comes to *The Plan,* there is no cookie, and there is no cutter. Custom-build your plan according to what you perceive is right for you and your career. That means your plan is as simple or complex as it needs to be.

Some of my clients are working from an incredibly rigorous plan. Others work from something rough, sometimes just a few hand-drawn charts. And while the format matters little, what matters is that your plan clearly outlines the steps you are taking in getting what you want.

THREE BEST PRACTICES

Before getting started on your plan, it's helpful to first develop the narrative for your career.

In a most remarkable book, *Presence*, co-author Betty Sue Flowers writes, "The scenario-planning work I've been doing at Shell has reminded me how important stories are in helping people make sense of a complex reality."

The same is true in your career.

Think about the story of your career as you developed it back in *Define It*. Look back on where your career has been. Project forward to your grandest vision.

What is the narrative behind the way you are driving your career? If you were sitting with me, how would you tell me the story of your career?

Where has it been? Where is it headed? Why does your vision matter so much to you?

Now, having done that, here are three best practices for developing your plan.

IF IT'S NOT ON PAPER, IT'S NOT A PLAN

You can't get in shape by imagining yourself exercising.

You might be tempted to skip through this section, integrating the ideas, but figuring you can get by without putting pen to paper or hands to keys.

But you are wrong! If it's not on paper, it's not a plan. It's a daydream.

Even if you just put a few boxes on a page, notice that there is something magical in taking the ideas swirling in your mind and writing them down.

This is where most people fail. How many of your colleagues, for instance, talk about what they maybe, sometime, possibly might do in their careers? A good number, I would bet. I would also bet that as long as you have known them, they have gone nowhere. They pretend that one day they will get to it, but because they never take the time to organize their ideas, they never get anywhere.

Do you really want to be hanging out with them for the rest of your life? Be different. Write it down.

PLAN WHAT YOU ARE WILLING TO DO

One big reason people fail to get value from planning is because they craft elaborate plans that they are unwilling to execute. Like a drunk idiot at a bar, their mouths write checks that their bodies can't cash.

In developing your plan, focus on what you are actually willing to do.

Rather than trying to hone in on *the* one and only career that is the most magnificent of your dreams, think about a dream career you are willing to create. If you have grand visions, you must be willing to put in grand efforts, and if your priorities are elsewhere—Twitter, *Game of Thrones*, whatever—then don't develop a plan that you will fail to put to work.

Develop your plan based on what you are willing to do.

And remember to keep it actionable. Your plan is not your dream. It is not your grandest vision for your career. Your plan consists of the steps you are taking for building your grandest vision. So focus on the steps you will actually take moving toward what you truly want.

FOR NOW, FORGET THE "HOW"

The purpose of your plan is not to figure out how you are going to get it all done. Rather, it is to spell out your ideas for taking actions.

If you are setting Big Hairy Audacious Goals that are beyond your current sight, you do not yet know how you will reach your goal. Rather, focus on laying out the steps you can identify, knowing that as you keep taking those steps, you will keep figuring out how you keep taking more steps.

You might not yet know how, for instance, you are getting promoted, yet by laying out your plan, you give yourself the focus and organization required for taking steps.

TWO STEPS TO PLAN IT

As I've said, there is no definitive format for your plan. I am sharing the approach I typically use. You can use a different format if you choose. (But I'm a crafty bugger, and I already had you take these two steps back in *Define It!*)

═══ STEP 1 ═══

VISUALIZE YOUR PLAN

Your plan becomes clearer when you look at it visually.

Think about the blueprint for a house. While words can be interpreted in different ways, a visual plan clearly and objectively represents the steps you will take. Even the most complex goals seem astonishingly manageable when they are visualized.

In divide and conquer, we began laying out your goals along separate workstreams for driving your career.

A ridiculously simple step, laying out your goals this way shows you the different ways for driving results. Like breaking down the revenue stream of a product company into volume and price shows you the drivers of revenue, breaking down your career into separate workstreams shows you how you keep driving your career.

1. YOUR EXTERNAL WORKSTREAM is commercial success—what you must do for driving your business.

2. YOUR INTERNAL WORKSTREAM is everything you are doing inside your company to get the support you need.

3. THE 3RD TRACK You!, is your personal, professional development track.

Simple, enough, right? All we have done is taken our goal to drive your career all the way to the top and broken it down into the separate work-streams. This is called divide and conquer. Next, we build it out. Here, you build the steps along each of your workstreams, thinking through the sequence of actions you need to take to get what you want. Simply and logically, ask: "What happens next?"

Going back to our example, let's build it out one more level.

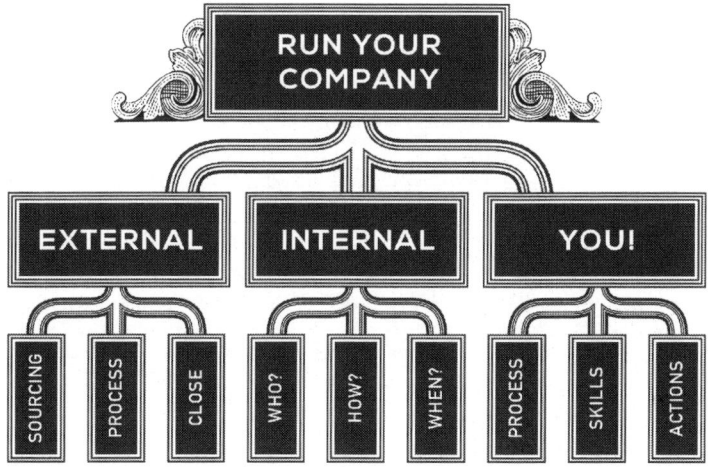

All we have done is add another level of detail by asking: "What's the next action?" This is a simple yet incredibly powerful tool for planning what you want.

Consider the internal workstream. We have taken this mess of a thing people think of as "having the right conversations" and "politics" and broken it down into three tracks for executing inside your company:

- *WHOM do you need to influence?*

- *HOW are they influenced?*

- *WHEN do you influence them?*

Then, from there, keep building out the "nodes," which will end up looking like the MPC framework that you will see in *Getting Paid and Promoted.* In a handful of steps, you develop a robust plan for influencing decision-makers inside your company.

Apply the same approach on your other two workstreams—build it out node-by-node, and lay out your visual plan for doing what you want.

For instance, let's go a step deeper on your external workstream, which is your path for driving commercial success.

Let's assume you are a salesperson focused on driving revenues. Previously we built three nodes for your external workstream: sourcing, process, and execution. Hence, you focus on:

- *HOW do I source clients?*

- *WHAT is my process for building relationships and for driving revenues?*

- *HOW do I close? That is, how do I go from calling on my accounts to generating revenues?*

Let's build out sourcing into more detail. Here, you ask: *How do I source potential clients?* While a mediocre salesperson might rely on pounding away in hopes of making progress, instead, bring deliberate intent and develop a highly sophisticated approach to sourcing.

Doing that, you might separate your list into three types of accounts.

1. THE FIRST NODE, "House," are the accounts with which you already have strong relationships. For this node, you might conclude that your role is deepening your relationship, serving your client, and positioning your firm for revenue opportunities.

2. THE SECOND NODE is "Green-field" opportunities, where you are developing relationships with under-served companies looking to build a relationship from the ground up.

3. THE THIRD TRACK, "Steal," is the most interesting and fun, so let's build it out a bit more.

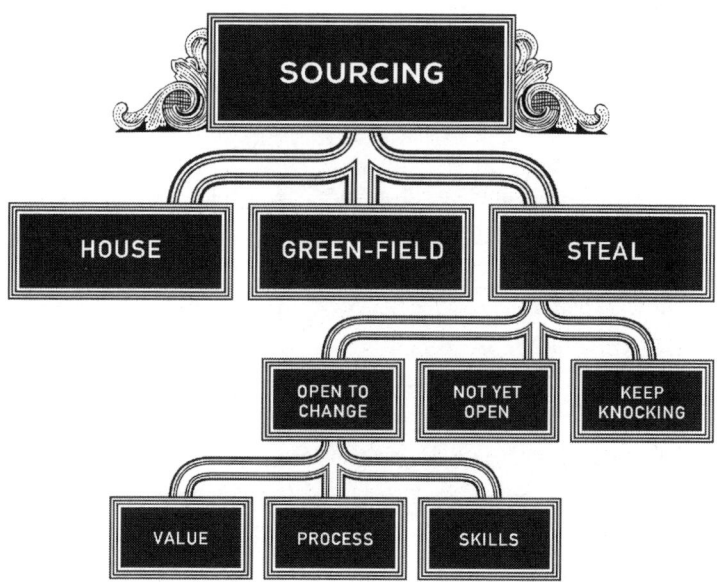

"Steal" is building relationships with clients who are house accounts of your competitors. Here you figure out how to out-compete and blow out your competition so that you can win their existing clients.

In targeting accounts, you might begin by assessing where it is worth spending your time, based on the likelihood of the customer's openness to making a change. After determining where you benefit in spending your time, we build it out one more level, this time focusing on how you penetrate these accounts and out-shine your competition.

On the first branch, you are focusing on the most important idea we have discussed—value. Here, you identify the ways you can provide massive value to your target customer. That goes far beyond showing up and pitching the same old stuff the same old way. It means going deep into their psyche and understanding what is of great value to them.

The next two branches relate to two other topics we have discussed throughout this guide. Namely, to penetrate and steal accounts, you must develop your process and skills. While your average salesperson might think building a relationship is just a matter of time, you instead want to develop an exceptional process designed to quickly and powerfully drive results. That requires skills. And I'm not just talking basic skills of selling or simply getting better at building rapport or influencing, I am talking about developing wickedly powerful people skills that enable you to quickly win over customers.

While my most advanced secret approaches are outside of the scope of this book (and you'll never see them in a book), I am going to share one of my methods for destroying your competition.

Let's say you want to steal a house account, and you walk into a meeting doing what your potential customer expects: You are critical of your competition.

Do you know what will happen? I do.

You will harm your credibility.

But what if you are highly complimentary of your competition, citing the great products or services they offer and how important loyalty is in building relationships. Then, while you are having a pleasing and somewhat un-expected conversation on one level, you can undermine and destroy your competition covertly by using non-verbal communications.

As you know, roughly eighty percent of communication is not the words you use. By becoming an expert in the skill of communication (see: *Getting Skills*), you can undermine your competitors in a variety of ways. You might use a slightly "dirty" tone. Or perhaps using a physical "anchor" in the room, you might casually gesture toward the trash container while talking about their "old" relationship.

Now, that all might seem like dirty boxing, but rather, you are out-com-peting your competitors by taking your skills to an entirely different level. And, of course, you will never win a client over by communications alone. You win clients by creating **massive value**.

Using advanced skills just gives you an opportunity to open their minds and show them that you deliver massive value.

══ STEP 2 ══

ACTION STEPS

At the end of *Define It,* you went to the step of laying out your workstreams on a basic timeline consisting of three timeframes: Now, in six to twelve months, and in two to three years.

Here, I suggest you go back to where you left off and this time develop a more comprehensive timeline, incorporating the specific steps associated with your different workstreams.

There are, of course, many ways you can lay out your plan and again, I suggest your plan is as simple as it needs to be in order to clearly define the steps you are now taking.

As you keep developing your timeline, it can be helpful to keep planning and revising by considering these four filters.

1. THE COMPLETION CYCLE. Think about your plan according to these three steps—initiation, action, and completion.

2. SEE YOUR PLAN AS A PROCESS. Consider sequencing, prioritization, lead times, critical path, dependent tasks, and so on.

3. APPLY SYSTEMS THINKING. When you think about any system, think about where that system moves smoothly and where there are potential problems. What speeds you up? What slows you down?

4. KEEP COMING BACK TO THE THREE LEVERS. Your plan happens through people, activities, and things. So keep asking: *What people do I need to engage? What activities need to happen? What things must be completed?*

Expanding on the table from *Timeline It* and incorporating these ideas, you might end up with a table like this one:

	CREATION	ACTION	COMPLETION	PEOPLE	ACTIVITIES	THINGS
EXTERNAL						
• SOURCING						
• PROCESS						
• CLOSE						
INTERNAL						
• WHO?						
• WHAT?						
• WHEN?						
YOU!						

Again, although I am keeping this incredibly simple and high level, you might spend weeks, months, and even years developing your highly sophisticated plan for doing what you want in your career. It is up to you. Build what you need for doing what you want.

With these two steps you should have a solid plan coming together. Now you have something to play with, let's play!

CHAPTER SIXTEEN

EXECUTE IT

A good plan violently executed now is better than a perfect

plan executed next week.

— GENERAL PATTON

★　　★　　★　　★　　★　　★

In 2000, after the Internet bubble burst, the rules of the game changed. Whereas in the go-go days, any dot-com could go public, investors became far more selective.

To go public, you had to be exceptional. You not only needed a great company story, but unlike the bubble days where you could go public off a business plan and a sniff of revenues, companies were required to have demonstrated strong operating and financial execution.

During a time few companies could go public, a network security company called NetScreen easily passed the test. A revolutionary company, NetScreen's hardware-based Internet security products were generations ahead of its giant rivals, Cisco and Nokia.

During the time I worked on the IPO, I would have told you that these innovative products were the secret to NetScreen's success.

But years later, I came to think differently.

It happened in my office in San Francisco while I was meeting a Hong Kong-based investor who wanted to discuss NetScreen in the context of an investment he had made in a similar company. Having never heard of his company, I presumed that it was not the caliber of NetScreen. Yet, as we talked, I learned that his company was founded around the same time. It too had invented similarly advanced ASIC-based security technology. NetScreen's products, it turned out, were not as ahead-of-the-competition as I had thought.

Here was the difference: While NetScreen had gotten to market with groundbreaking products, his company had spent years longer in the lab. And while years later, his company was still run by its founders, NetScreen's investors and founders brought in a world-class management team as soon as it could afford to do so. This team took a great technology and built a great company.

That day, I realized that NetScreen's secret of success was not in its superior technology, but due to aggressive and flawless execution. The same is true in putting to work this guide. Your plan doesn't get you what you want. Rather, it's what you do with it from here.

As Leonardo da Vinci said, "I have been impressed with the urgency of doing. Knowing is not enough; we must apply. Being willing is not enough; we must do."

4
EXECUTE
IT

If you are reading this guide, I know you are already someone who takes action. To have successfully made it to a good job, execution is something you know how to do.

That is why I expect you will find *Execute It* to be one of the easiest steps in this guide. In fact, because you are already good at executing, rather than focusing on what more you can do, instead, we are asking: What less can you do?

Thoreau wrote, "Simplify, simplify, simplify." In *Execute It*, I set out to develop a simple approach to execution, which works in two steps.

But first, I want to discuss something that might be relevant to you.

ARE YOU MOVING?

The book *Unstoppable* tells the story of Legson Kayira. In 1958, sixteen-year-old Kayira set off from his small tribal village in East Africa to walk three thousand miles to Cairo, where he resolved to board a ship for America and get a college education. With little idea how this would happen and with only five days' supply of food, he began his journey.

Five days later, he was out of food and had only covered twenty-five miles. Inspired by stories of men like Abraham Lincoln, he vowed to keep going or die trying. A full fifteen months later, having crossed dangerous tribal lands and survived a deadly fever, he had walked one thousand miles to Uganda. He still had a long way to go, but having come so far, his resolve had strengthened.

As he walked, stories of his journey spread, which led him to be accepted into an American college, where the students even raised money to pay for his airfare. Legson went on to become a successful writer and a professor of political science at the esteemed Cambridge University.

I know transformational results do not always happen quickly, and while putting this guide to work is far easier than walking three thousand miles to Cairo, I share Legson's story as a reminder of the power of having a great vision and simply taking one step at a time.

Having come this far both in your career and in reading this guide, *Execute It* is simply about taking the small steps to keep moving forward. In this way, it's more like renovating a house while you stay inside. Your career is already built. You are just taking steps.

Austrian philosopher Otto Neurath said it well, "We are like sailors who must rebuild their ship on the open sea, never able to dismantle it in drydock and to reconstruct it there out of the best materials."

Wherever you are in your career, now is the time to take steps putting this guide to work. There will never come some thundering to take action—other than now. If you keep thinking one day that time will arrive, you will likely be standing in the same place still looking forward.

So, if you have not been taking action, just take a step. Any step. Script up and have one conversation that is designed to feed-forward your performance. Take action on just one task that drives your commercial success. Read anything, even just a quote that gets you fired up about getting what you want. What step you take matters little. Just take a step or two.

That is the only way you will get what you want. As Henry Ford said, "Vision without execution is just hallucination."

THE SKILL OF EXECUTION

Think of execution not as something you do, but as a skill. In fact, as I will discuss next in *Getting Skills*, you can think of all the topics we cover as skills. This implies that anyone can learn these skills, and it also becomes obvious that once you learn the skill, you can apply it to everything you do.

The skill of execution works the same way. It's a skill of taking action with everything you do, including putting your plan to work.

To execute your plan, I suggest breaking it into two modes: "what?" (which is everything that needs to get done) and "you!" (which is what you must be able to do).

WHAT IS WHAT?

"What?" represents everything that needs to happen, such as activities that need to take place and things that need to get done.

For instance, in our example of running your company, we built out three workstreams—external, internal, and you! Then, imagining yourself in the role of a salesperson we built in detail a number of steps relating to building client relationships.

In doing that, we implied a series of activities that need to take place, such as setting up meetings, and those meetings leading to business.

In *Execute It*, you add specificity to the activities and things that need to happen, and then you take action.

Another aspect to "what?" is recognizing that execution always happens at multiple levels. At a micro level, execution refers to the meetings you set up and the relationships you further. At a macro level, every meeting and every relationship is one more step toward building your commercial success. In this way, you clearly see how every step you take with every client has you executing your external workstream. So by taking steps every day, you are executing the small steps that drive your plan.

Similarly, while taking steps on your external workstream, inside your firm, you are also advancing your internal workstream. In build it out, we identified the *who?, what?,* and *when?* of your internal conversations. In *Execute It,* you develop your scripts, schedule those meetings, and execute. Again, these action steps are powerfully executing your plan.

YOU!

If you think of "what?" as all the activities and things that need to happen, think of "you!" as the person who is doing them!

THAT MEANS TWO THINGS.

1. FIRST, IT MEANS KNOWING WHAT TO DO.

2. SECOND, IT MEANS BEING ABLE TO DO IT.

Notice the difference between the two. Knowing what to do is one thing, but being able to do it is an entirely different beast. And, ultimately, that's the crux of "you!"

Can you actually take the steps of *Execute It?* Who do you need to be to successfully *Execute It?*

For instance, if your goal is your process of being promoted to run your company, do you have what it takes to lead? Do you have the experience? Do you have the various skills you need to be an effective leader? If not, who must you become?

What does that mean for you and your goals? Which version of you is capable of executing your plan? What are the personal attributes that enable you to execute it and get what you want? How will you succeed where others fail?

While it is common to think about execution in terms of what you must do, in fact, *Execute It* is much more personal.

Take a moment to think about that now. Go back to the ideas we covered in *Starting With You.* Are you applying the performance tools and becoming who you need to be to successfully execute your plan and get what you want?

THE FIVE PRINCIPLES OF EXCELLENT EXECUTION

Evangelist and motivational speaker Robert Schuller said, "High achievers spot rich opportunities swiftly, make big decisions quickly, and move into action immediately. Follow these principles and you can make your dreams come true."

He was making some good points, but let's explore execution more deeply by reviewing my five principles of excellent execution.

GET STARTED

In 1983, the *Journal of American Physics* published a discovery that a domino fall could not only topple many things, but it could topple much bigger things.

So in 2001, a physicist from San Francisco's Exploratorium tested the theory by creating eight dominoes out of plywood, each of which was fifty percent larger than the previous. His first domino was a mere two-inches. His last was roughly three-feet tall. Getting started with a gentle touch, the final domino fell with an enormous thud!

Hence, Principle 1: What begins as one small step can have a much larger and increasing impact. You can plan forever, but magic happens when you get started.

Think about that for a moment. How many of your dreams have you taken action on? When was the last time? What happened when you got started taking action? What lessons did you learn then that you can apply now?

The key is to begin one step at a time. Surely you have heard the saying, "Your eyes are bigger than your stomach." With too much on your plate, not only do you risk not getting finished, but you risk becoming overwhelmed and never getting started. So break your plan into manageable steps and bite off the right amount so you walk and chew.

Then, do what Nike says, and just do it! There's enormous power in just doing it. In just taking steps, you will find yourself getting motivated and excited, and like any runner who hates the first ten minutes of a run, once you get moving, it's pure joy.

PROCESS EXCELLENCE

Execution is about process. It's about knowing the steps to take and being good at taking them. Like a good production line, good execution comes from good process. Therefore, excellent execution comes from excellent process.

In executing your plan, the rules of process excellence apply: sequencing, prioritization, efficiency, effectiveness, and the like. Develop a process for putting your plan to work. For example, three of my clients meet with me on Sunday nights. By getting together before their week takes off, they are preparing themselves, organizing their week, and planning what needs to be executed so that they can move forward and execute their plans.

From there, keep refining your process of execution through continuous improvement. Ask yourself: *How can I can get better at my process of execution? What can I do differently? Better? Faster?*

Remember when I said that your plan is an iterative process? This is because at every stage of your process, you must consider how to continuously improve so that you can get what you want. And that's where it really counts, right? It's not whether you are getting started, nor whether you are continuously improving your process, but whether you are executing your process all the way to the end.

Consider yourself a tight rope walker. You might take a breather along the way, but never rest your attention until your feet are firmly planted on other side.

MOMENTUM

Newton's first law of motion states that an object in motion stays in motion with the same speed and in the same direction unless acted upon by an unbalanced force.

The same is true with excellent execution. Getting started gets you in motion, and from there, putting your plan to work and getting what you want is all about continuing the momentum.

If you are not aggressively pushing forward, it is likely you are sliding backward and excellent execution requires continually taking steps to keep up the momentum.

Momentum comes from constantly charging forward, continuously improving your process of execution, and keeping your energy moving in the right direction. One way of doing this is by designing your execution in such a way that you can achieve small victories along the way. So, as you keep moving forward, use your successes to give you the momentum to keep taking steps.

For instance, one of my clients is focused on raising $1 billion of capital. At first that might seem daunting, but by breaking it down and seeing that he might get there with just ten $100 million dollar investments or one hundred $10 million dollar investments, it becomes obvious that every meeting is moving him closer to his goal.

You can apply this idea toward any goal simply by asking: *How can I see my goal as a series of smaller victories that are enabling me to build momentum?*

PERSISTENCE

Keeping up the momentum is important, but what is even more important is keeping it up for as long as it takes, which is potentially indefinitely.

I once asked a client, a former Navy SEAL what the difference is between those who "Drop-On-Request" during Hell Week and ring the brass bell and the select few who make it all the way through.

What do you think he said?

Skills? Nope.

Mindset? Nope.

He said that it's only one thing: The will to keep going.

It's going to the point where your mind has long given up and your body just keeps going. It is persistence and grit. It is the same thing that motivates a marathon runner to finish the race with two bloody feet. Of course, executing your plan is not that painful or dramatic, but to be sure, excellent execution requires great persistence.

So how do you motivate yourself to have that type of persistence? You can beat your chest and yell Nike slogans, which might be effective, but that can feel hard. It is the stuff of heart attacks and anger management classes.

Besides, it might take you many years to put your plan to work. And if you are gritting your teeth and holding onto the pull-up bar just a little harder because you have to, you are going to give up at some point. It is inevitable.

To keep yourself moving takes a whole lot more than simple grit.

When famous operatic tenor Luciano Pavarotti was asked how he persisted in working so long to stay at the top of his game, he said, "People think I'm disciplined. It is not discipline. It is devotion. There is a great difference."

When you are devoted to your plan, it becomes easy to persist. One way is knowing why your goals matter to you. That way, not only are you willing to do what it takes, but you love doing what it takes.

======= PRINCIPLE 5 =======

PROPULSION SYSTEM

When you have a big enough "why," excellent execution comes easily. Executing your plan will never feel like something you begrudgingly have to do, but rather it will be what you absolutely love to do.

Principle 5 is a fancy way of saying, "Motivation." But in this case, think of motivation in two powerful ways.

Close your eyes and imagine you are at your desk whining about how you do not have time to create the life you truly want. Then imagine that The Joker walks up behind you, slides a blade in your mouth, and gives you two choices: Either take five steps of your plan, or he carves a permanent smile on your face.

Do you think that might get you moving?

Now imagine the opposite. What if I suggest that a magic genie will appear and grant you any three wishes you desire once you complete five steps? Do you think that might help you find a little time to take a few steps?

These two ideas form your propulsion system. Remember that you are both moving away from what you don't want and toward what you do what.

This is the dirty secret to *Execute It.* It's quite simple really: Execution is easy if you both want it enough and the pain of not achieving it is bad enough.

Think about anything you have ever truly wanted, and how eagerly you went out there to make it happen. Think about why you did that—why that goal was so important to you—and the motivators that propelled you to take action.

Apply those motivators that worked so well in your past to what you want today and see them in action for you. Getting you one step closer, then another, and another, all the way until you are kicking back and tasting the sweet smell of getting what you want.

ONTO THE NEXT

If you go back to where we started on *The Plan,* you will remember that we have been working through the two steps of your plan: *Plan It* and *Execute It.* In finishing up *Execute It,* we've covered the first four process steps of *The System.*

Throughout this guide, I have explained that getting what you want requires a combination of two things: process and skills. Having finished the first four process steps, now we get into the second component and fifth and final step of *The System,* which is *Getting Skills.*

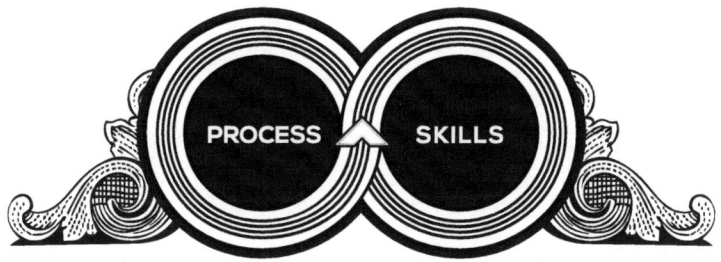

Having defined your process and laid out your steps for getting what you want, consider that you have two ways of thinking of which to choose.

One way says, "Well, I am who I am, so it's just a matter of how I go about doing this."

The other way is to ask yourself: *If I am serious about getting what I want, what skills must I develop?*

Doing what you want is as much about executing on the process steps as it is about becoming the person who can achieve your goals. Rather than simply taking steps, see how in becoming the person capable of taking your steps, success is inevitable.

CHAPTER SEVENTEEN

GETTING SKILLS

Formal education will make you a living; self-education will make you a fortune.

— JIM ROHN

★　★　★　★　★　★

"If you say it is about process and skills, what matters most?"

He is challenging me, barely glancing up from the page.

"What do you mean?" I ask.

He fires back, "I mean exactly what I said. If you think you can teach me something, then what matters most: process or skills?"

I laugh, turn my body to one side and place my left hand over the right, changing the tone.

"There is no 'matters most,'" I say. "Consider your superior company performance: Do you have a superior business *process,* or is it that your *skills* are superior?"

"What do you mean?" he asks.

Parroting his tone, I fire back, "I mean exactly what I said."

This time, he laughs. I got him.

Consider UFC fighter Jon Jones. He is the ultimate fighter for good reason. Standing inches from his opponent, ducking and weaving, his opponent's shots barely glance his ear. He rarely gets caught, and it is because he knows the process and he has the skills.

To be exceptional, you must be expert at both the process of your craft and the skills incumbent to it. From training camp to fight plan, Jones studies tapes and custom-builds his approach to exploiting his opponent's weaknesses and bringing the fight to him. A pro, Jones has his process down cold.

But with that alone, he would lose. He wins because he combines his rigorous process with surgical-precision and hard-hitting skills.

"You are an exceptional leader," I say. "But driving your company to the next level requires going beyond what you were capable of doing in the past and developing new skills."

He smiles. I turn my body back toward him, open up my arms and place them on the chair, once again changing the tone. He catches me and laughs. This time he knows exactly what I have done. Already, he's learning advanced skills of communications, and so too are you.

EVERYTHING IS A SKILL

In Upgrade U, Beyoncé sings to Jay-Z, "I hear you be the block but I'm the lights that keep the streets on," and in *The System*, process and skills come together the same way.

Although *Getting Skills* is shown as the final step in *The System*, your process and skills have been coming together all along.

In every step of *The System*, you gain or improve your skills. In *Define It,* you developed, among other things, the skill of goal setting. In *Getting It,* you built the skill of strategy—stepping back, thinking three chess moves ahead, like a Grandmaster building the skills for taking the last piece. In *Plan It* and *Execute It,* you enhanced your skills of planning and executing.

And throughout this guide, you are building a much more potent skill: The skill of doing what you want!

Like a lumberjack can chop down a tree with an axe, you have developed the essential tools. But like handing the lumberjack a chainsaw and seeing how much more he can do, I want to hand you the power tools. These are four skills that massively increase your impact and when paired with the process steps, powerfully propel you forward.

But before covering the power tools, let's talk more generally about how you quickly and powerfully build the skills you need for doing what you want.

CHAPTER EIGHTEEN

THE SYSTEM FOR LEARNING

Anyone who stops learning is old, whether at twenty or eighty. Anyone who keeps learning stays young.

— HENRY FORD

★　★　★　★　★　★

S ay you want to become excellent at the skill of negotiation. You might pick up a few great books, like *Getting To Yes* and *Negotiation,* and you begin working your way through. If you have never learned the basic skill of speed reading, you will read at the average rate of 250 words per minute, and you will likely take a month to get through those books.

And by the time you are done, you will remember only about five percent of what you read.

If you are diligent, you might have highlighted or dog-eared some pages, clipped from your Kindle, or written some notes, but how do you take all the time you have invested in reading to develop your skill of negotiation?

And what if you want to get better and better? The better you want to be, the bigger the challenge becomes.

That is the problem I faced for many years. I worked through hundreds of books on skills, summarizing and creating thousands pages of notes. But none of the books I read gave me a process for taking those ideas and developing skills. And while I occasionally flicked through my notes, in getting serious about learning skills, I knew I needed a rigorous process.

But first, I needed to identify the skills I needed to learn.

THE SEVEN LIFE SKILLS

What are the most important skills for creating the life I truly want and how do I learn them?

When I asked myself this question, I began generalizing, organizing, and categorizing different skills to determine what I believe are the most impactful skills for doing what you want. I call these the seven life skills.

If you develop at least proficiency at each of these skills, and you continually apply them in all facets of your life, then not only will you create more success, but you will also live a much richer life.

While developing the skill of communication will likely create more success in your career, it will also greatly improve the quality of your life. For instance, the number one reason cited for divorce is poor communication, so imagine how much richer your life would be if you mastered the skill of communication?

So how do you learn these skills?

THE PROCESS OF LEARNING

Aristotle said, "What we have to learn to do, we learn by doing."

Think about the ways you have learned all things. Consider the way you learned in school. It was not from sitting in class listening to your teachers drone on or from reading thousands of pages of books. You learned by taking knowledge and putting it to work.

That required making use of vast amounts of knowledge. You needed to determine what knowledge was of value, then capture, frame, analyze, and condense it concisely for writing papers and developing study notes. Cramming for exams, you learned through review and repetition.

It was not through the teaching that you learned. It was from what you did with the knowledge that led to learning. All learning works the same way. You learn by taking knowledge and converting it into practices.

This is what I call the process of learning. It works in three simple steps.

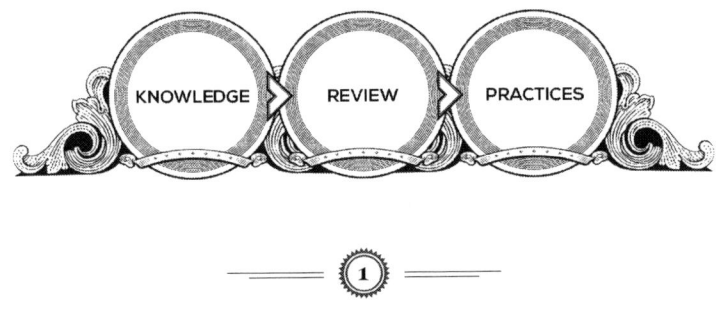

ACCUMULATE KNOWLEDGE

The first step to learning is to accumulate knowledge. You might learn by hiring a coach, by reading or listening to books, or by attending a workshop.

REVIEW

This means that you develop a process for reviewing your knowledge. This is, of course, analogous to how you organized study notes at school.

PRACTICES

Because you learn through doing, it is crucial that you take your knowledge and review and develop your practices. This process of converting knowledge into practices is the most important step for getting skills.

Think of it like the way Daniel-san learned karate. At first, Mr. Miyagi didn't train Daniel-san to punch and kick. Daniel-san developed his skill of karate through repetitive practice of household chores: painting the fence, waxing the car, and the like.

The same is true when one learns to sing. You, in fact, spend little time actually singing. You spend most of your time loosening up your voice, practicing scales, and developing the practices that are developing your skill of singing.

That's exactly what the process of learning is built to do. It works by giving you a structure for putting knowledge to practice. With this process, and through repetition, you can take your skills as far as you want to go.

PRACTICE ALL THE WAY
TO MASTERY

Bruce Lee said, "I fear not the man who has practiced 10,000 kicks once, but I fear the man who has practiced one kick 10,000 times."

Here's what he meant: With repetitive practice, you can quickly take your skills all the way to mastery. Conceptualize this idea by seeing yourself climbing the competence ladder, which shows your natural progression in learning skills.

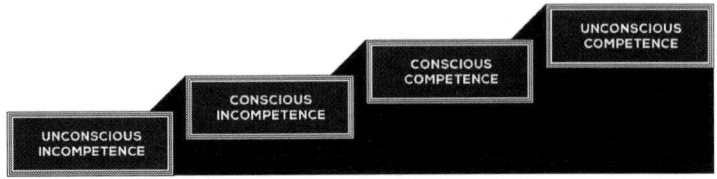

1. UNCONSCIOUS INCOMPETENCE happens before you even know you should start learning. As my client says, "The first step to learning is accepting you are terrible at something."

2. THAT'S WHAT GETS YOU TO THE NEXT STEP: CONSCIOUS IN-COMPETENCE. In this step, you are aware that you are incompetent, and you take steps to improve yourself. Here you are accumulating knowledge, doing your review and practices, and stepping up to conscious competence.

3. WITH CONSCIOUS COMPETENCE, you have developed the skill, but like learning to drive a car, you are required to think about what you are doing.

4. THEN, THROUGH REPETITION, as you keep practicing your skills, you reach the fourth step: **Unconscious Competence**. Like driving a car, you have now mastered the skill to the point you can do it without thinking. This is true mastery and what you are working toward.

While the notion of unconscious competence might seem somewhat abstract as applied to your career, in fact, I would bet that you have proven it many times already. Just look at the way you have already mastered a range of skills associated to your job. Whatever your level and career you can most certainly see that tasks that once required your full attention you now complete on auto-pilot. All skills develop the same way.

LEARNING THE POWER TOOLS

Even if he is continuously sharpening his saw, a lumberjack can hack at a tree all day. But when he picks up a chainsaw, he has far more impact.

Impact is what matters when a boxer throws a punch. When he hits the bag, he punches all the way through. In the ring, he has a limited supply of energy and lands a fraction of the punches he throws. He has to make every shot count and land every punch with devastating impact.

You want the same in your career.

While the seven life skills are highly effective in creating the life you truly want, there are four skills—what I call the power tools—that have the most impact in most professional careers.

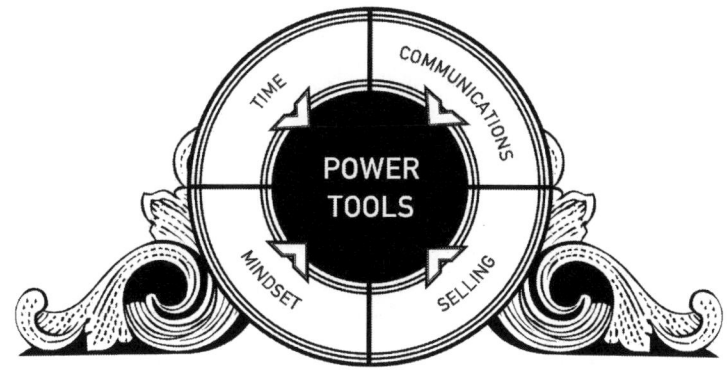

This is not to say these are the only or even the most important skills for you to learn, and I suggest carefully considering the skills that are most impactful for you in your career and then building a process for learning these skills.

We cover these skills briefly, but do not be fooled. Bringing all these ideas together in teaching you the power tools, I am sharing a small number of moves that have annihilating impact.

I am not teaching you the stuff you will find reading a few books. I am teaching you the skills I figured out from reading hundreds of books—and summarizing them. And then developing summaries and summaries of summaries. And hunting down teachers to learn the things you will never find in a book.

Also, I am able to teach you the power tools briefly and quickly because we are relying on two powerful concepts you have already learned.

First, we are using the process of learning. Right away, I am condensing the knowledge and only sharing with you a basic review, focusing on what you need to know and the practices for right now putting these skills to work.

Second, putting to work the idea we covered in *Getting It*, I am not just teaching you any knowledge, I am teaching you the dominant ideas—the five principles that powerfully drive each of these skills.

CHAPTER NINETEEN

THE SKILL OF TIME MANAGEMENT

Just a few words on time management:
Forget all about it.

— TIMOTHY FERRISS IN *THE 4-HOUR WORKWEEK*

★　★　★　★　★　★

There are people out there who are experts at time management. They have all these processes and workflows, lists, folders and sub-folders, yellow Post-its, and blue ones too.

But where many get time management wrong is when they make it out to be this "thing" you have to do. You are told you must complete boring, laborious, painful tasks—like scheduling and labeling. You must discipline yourself to squeeze more into your day. Time management is seen by others as creating efficiency and effectiveness through productivity tips.

I suggest seeing it differently.

Time management is life management. You already manage your time every second of your day. Building your skill of time management means that you bring a deliberate approach to allocating your time. Thought of like this, time management is not about what you *have* to do. It is about taking control of your time and doing more of what you *want* to do.

You want to spend less time doing the things you do not enjoy and more time doing the things you do enjoy. Also, you want to get maximum benefit from every minute you sell to your company by having hard-hitting impact in everything you do. You can do that by allocating more time where you have more impact and by driving more "yield," driving more value per unit of your time.

Then it is up to you whether you choose to work the same or more hours and drive more value, or to work fewer hours and drive the same value. However you see it, the skill of time management is getting more of the time of your life.

THE PRINCIPLES OF TIME MANAGEMENT

You can read hundreds of books and millions of productivity tips about time management, but most of them are a waste of time and easily captured by my five principles.

══════ PRINCIPLE 1 ══════

MAKE ACTIVE CHOICES

Time management is priority management. As time management guru David Allen says, "You can do anything, but not everything."

While it is common to see time management as squeezing in as much as possible, I suggest figuring out what matters to you and stop doing everything else. Rather than going with the flow and using your time as others might want, instead choose to focus your time where you want.

Making active choices means that you prioritize, delegate, know what you do and don't do, and distinguish between that which is urgent and that which is important—ultimately use your time as you choose.

══════ PRINCIPLE 2 ══════

SHIFT YOUR TIME TO ITS HIGHEST-VALUE USE

"Shift your time to its highest-value use" might be the only principle you need on time management. It replaces all the random tips and ideas you hear like "close your email, forward your phone, and stop multi-tasking."

Imagine you are in your office preparing for a meeting that begins in one hour. You are reading your notes and organizing your thoughts when you hear that "ding." You look up to read your email.

A colleague is asking a question and has requested an urgent response. Your response is complicated, and you begin crafting a somewhat lengthy reply.

Then it strikes you: Your colleague does not own your time.

Your colleague does not determine whether you should give an urgent response. You determine that your pressing meeting is a more urgent and a higher-value use of your time, so you go back to preparing.

You put this principle to work through practice. Many of us are so conditioned to let others make demands on our time that we must constantly ask ourselves questions like, "Who says this is important? To whom does it matter whether I complete this task now or later?"

In applying this principle, you choose the highest-value use of your time. Which is the highest-value use of your time: Watching the game on a Sunday or getting an early start on your week?

It's your call. Recharging by watching the game might very well be the highest use of your time, and recharging is important. When you are applying this principle, you are the one who chooses how to use your time.

PRINCIPLE 3

DO WHAT YOU CHOOSE

Time management is about sticking to your choices. Some might call this discipline or willpower, but that is a limited view relative to seeing it as a choice. Like stopping yourself from eating ice cream might take willpower, living inside the feeling of being in great shape makes your choice easy.

The best way to train doing what you choose is through repetition. Your brain is a muscle that you train. Just like it becomes easier and easier to lift weight through repetition, it becomes easier and easier to resist temptation through practice. In this way, willpower is a myth: It's not that one person has more willpower than another; it's that one person has more practice exercising willpower than another.

Imagine you are closely reading this guide, and just as you are getting really enthralled, you hear the "ding." You feel the urge to check your email, but you resist. You still want to check it, but you resist some more, telling yourself all the reasons reading this guide is important. Do that repeatedly and guess what happens a week from today when you hear the "ding"?

Your brain will be trained and the choice will be easy.

PRINCIPLE 4

FOCUS AND CONCENTRATION

This is from a *Forbes* article on one of my favorite billionaires, Sean Parker:

> *"When focused on a task, he blocks everything else out and works himself into a trance. The outside world fades; time slips away. 'It requires a lot of rescheduling, but I try to focus on things that are the highest-value and get those done perfectly.'"*

By far, the most important attribute to success is focusing on a task long enough to get it done, and done well.

While many of us consider ourselves excellent multi-taskers, every study, article, or talk on multi-tasking proves you wrong. Multi-tasking is simply a way of doing a number of things poorly at the same time. Not only does it ruin your ability to focus on one task, but by task-switching you are also destroying about eighty percent of your efficiency. That might sound ludicrously high, so let me explain how task-switching annihilates your productivity.

When the "ding" goes off and you check your email, you lose far more than the time you are diverting to the low-value task. Forced to think about a different topic, and likely in a different frame of mind, by the time you return to your original task, you not only must get back in the right frame of mind but also get back to where you left off. Do that all day every day, and imagine how much time you are burning.

So stop. Focus. Get more of your time!

—— PRINCIPLE 5 ——

MORE THAN A FEELING

You know that good feeling you get from clearing your inbox? To be sure, looking at a cleared inbox at the end of the day or week is a great feeling. And that's the problem. Chasing that great feeling of completion, you are inclined to focus on a low-value task rather than putting your time to a high-value task that will remain incomplete.

Einstein said, "Put your hand on a hot stove for a minute, and it seems like an hour. Sit with a pretty girl for an hour, and it seems like a minute. That is relativity." The same is true in time management.

Because it feels good to do certain things, such as getting tasks completed, you can be led to make bad choices in allocating your time. Instead, you are making better choices by putting this principle to work and bringing emotional intelligence to time management.

For instance, imagine instead of chasing the good feeling of clearing your inbox, you bring forward the good feeling of how an extra thirty minutes focused on putting this guide to work is getting you what you want.

THE PRACTICES OF TIME MANAGEMENT

Here are my top five practices for mastering time management.

PRACTICE 1

DO REGULAR TIME AUDITS

To know if you are using your time in the right way, you must first know how you are using your time. Do this by conducting regular time audits.

While it's easy to skip this practice, I assure you that everyone I have known who has done a time audit is shocked by the results. You can do this in as much detail as you choose using apps like Rescue Time, but with my clients, we typically do this in broad strokes, in a simple spreadsheet, keeping track of how you are using your time.

This will allow you to measure how you spend your time and give you the context to make better choices in the future. Also, because a task will typically take as much time as you allocate, a time audit gives you a powerful tool for planning your time in the future.

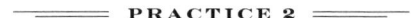

PRACTICE 2

PRIORITIZE IMPORTANT OVER URGENT

In my favorite book on time management, *Eat That Frog*, Brian Tracy writes: "There is never enough time to do everything, but there is always enough time to do the most important thing."

I often wrongly assume that everyone is aware of this time management practice. It is easy for our days to be consumed with what seems urgent—e.g., a time-stamped email, putting out fires—but this leaves us little time to get done what's important:

- BEGIN YOUR DAY with what is urgent and important.

- MOVE to what is important but not urgent.

- FINISH your day with what is urgent but not important.

- FORGET about all the tasks that are neither important nor urgent!

A specific example to consider is the way you read newspapers and other information sources. Rather than reading in detail in the morning, you might quickly scan to determine if there is anything important and urgent, and then come back to the rest of it later, if at all.

PRACTICE 3

USE "DO NOW" AND "DON'T-DO" LISTS

You are best organized when you put tasks directly in your calendar and on your "do now" list, which is just another way of naming your "to-do" list so that you actually do the task!

Another list, which is equally important but often overlooked is a "don't-do" list on which you clearly define the tasks you never do. For instance, as a senior executive, you might put all junior-level work that isn't directly related to driving your business on your don't-do list.

Here's one thing I suggest all my clients put at the top of their don't-do list: Stop reading useless junk. You would never read the back of a cereal box as you are throwing it in the trash, so why read most of the stuff you find in newspapers, magazines, or the Internet? A quick scan of high-value sources is all you need to determine if there is anything worthy of your time.

PRACTICE 4

PLAN AHEAD

By far the best way to practice time management is by planning your day. If you tick through all of the principles, you see each of them is easy to implement when you clearly define how you plan to use your time.

Planning enables you to practice your focus and concentration. For instance, I suggest my clients set aside hours when their assistant checks their email and derails all but the urgent phone call. And rather than having an open door policy, I suggest they set aside hours to be available and train others in the practice of focusing their time.

The best practice for planning ahead is setting aside a few minutes of deliberate thinking every morning. As Victor Hugo said, "He who every morning plans the transactions of that day and follows that plan carries a thread that will guide him through the labyrinth of the most busy life."

PRACTICE 5

MIND THE GAP

A top executive coach suggested my busy client spend forty-five minutes a day meditating. With similarly useless suggestions, he fired the coach and came to me looking for better answers. I taught him a series of mental training tools he can use in thirty seconds to a couple of minutes.

DO WHAT YOU WANT

That's what I mean by "Mind The Gap." It's not about using big blocks of time to accomplish tasks, this practice is about more efficiently using those small gaps of time you find available.

Find productive ways to use those first five minutes you are waiting for a call to start, or ten minutes when you are between meetings, or a few minutes amidst a busy schedule.

You might struggle to carve out big blocks of time, but you can use the small blocks of time all day that might aggregate to a few hours a week.

CHAPTER TWENTY

THE SKILL OF COMMUNICATION

Various scientific studies have proven that if you learn how to deal with other people, you will have gone about 85 percent of the way down the road to success in any business, occupation, or profession, and about 99 percent of the way down the road to personal happiness.

— LES GOBLIN

★   ★   ★   ★   ★   ★

You cannot not communicate. You are communicating with yourself and others every moment of every day. So when gauging how much the skill of communication can improve your life, I suggest the answer is: drastically!

By monitoring and changing your own internal communication, you can improve the way you feel and the actions you take—and not just by a little.

In upgrading your communication at home, you can better your relationships with your spouse and kids—and not just by a little.

What about in your career? If your skill of communication is the vehicle you use for getting anything and everything done in your job, how can training your skill drive more success in your career?

How can it not?

Unfortunately, like many skills, people often think of communication as an innate talent, something you either have or do not have. So they fail to train it. Yet, not only is the skill of communication one that everyone benefits from training, it is also incredibly easy to develop.

Think of it this way: You learned to speak before you were five years of age, so imagine how much you can improve upon a skill you learned as a baby! And unlike the years it took you to learn to speak as a baby, the skill of communication is easy to learn when done the right way.

Rather than reading a bunch of books, you only need a small number of top ideas you can practice over and over again.

But just because we are keeping it simple does not mean we are keeping it basic. Here, I will share some of the most advanced tools and powerful ideas I have learned from hundreds of books and from becoming a certified trainer of the most advanced tools.

Bringing these ideas together, I am not providing you with typical tools, but rather with the powerful underlying conscious and unconscious processes for driving communications.

THE PRINCIPLES OF COMMUNICATION

Barack Obama is a good example. Watch him speak, and in his words and gestures and overall process of communication, you will see many of the principles.

While he's a good orator, he excels at understanding the underlying drivers of communication and reaching his audience on multiple levels.

Understand, as he does, how your words move others, and you too will quickly and powerfully master the skill of communication.

PRINCIPLE 1

IT'S ABOUT THEM

Abraham Lincoln said, "When I am getting ready to reason with a man, I spend one-third of my time thinking about myself and what I am going to say and two-thirds about him and what he is going to say."

Powerful communication is not about you or your message. Powerful communication is about how your message is received by your audience.

Consider the difference between a husband saying, "I don't feel like you are listening to me," versus a husband who says, "I'm obviously at fault because I am failing to make myself clear." Guess which communication gets him a night on the sofa?

Rather than thinking about how your communication makes you feel, imagine seeing the world through the eyes of your audience and communicating in a manner that makes them feel the way you want them to feel.

This requires communicating with your audience on their level. Like communicating well in Paris means that you are speaking French, if all you speak is corporate-speak, you are unlikely to communicate well in a bar in Tennessee. By paying attention to your audience—listening, watching, and profiling—you are able to tailor your communication.

PRINCIPLE 2

AN EXPERIENCE

One of the great voices of contemporary literature, Dr. Maya Angelou, said, "I have learned that people will forget what you said, people will forget what you did, but people will never forget how you made them feel."

A reason we love to read great literature is because beautiful writers have a way of taking you on a journey. More than words on a page, they are giving you an experience. Like watching an engrossing film, you drift into their words, a part of the experience unfolding in front of you.

Communication works the same way. When you tell someone about your weekend, you can throw them bland words like a hack pitcher, or you can take them on a fun adventure. A politician trying to win an election can either drone on about boring policy details or can paint a picture of a country we all want to live in.

In every conversation, you are already taking people on an adventure, so ask yourself: *Is it an experience you would want more of?*

UNDERLYING PROCESS

You know those fighting movies that *always* come down to the last fight scene. That scene always plays out a certain way, right?

The good guy wins for a bit, then he starts losing, and he gets pushed to his brink before he gets an image of something heart-wrenching, like his daughter smiling at him. He gets inspired and throws the winning punch. Right?

What you see is that no matter what punches or kicks are thrown, there's always an underlying process to the scene.

The same is true in communications. It's not the content or the words that drive effective communications, but the underlying process, the structure by which you communicate.

For instance, for every meeting, my clients use a process that looks like this:

1. INTENT: Know your goal.

2. CHARACTER: Choose whom you must be to influence your audience.

3. STATE: Know what emotional state drives your audience.

4. TOOLS & SKILLS: Prepare your tools and skills.

No matter what the content, they are constantly coming back to the process of communication, ensuring they keep achieving their goals.

DRIVE STATE, DRIVE ACTIONS

As you now know, thoughts drive feelings and feelings drive actions. Therefore, in effectively communicating your message and driving your audience to take your desired actions, you must drive their emotional state.

Antoine de Saint-Exupéry, the wonderful French author, once wrote, "If you want to build a ship, don't drum up the men to gather wood, divide the work and give orders. Instead, teach them to yearn for the vast and endless sea."

Imagine thinking of all your communications in the same way. Rather than intending to drive home a certain message, step back and ask yourself what emotion must you inspire in your audience to get them to take the actions you want. Do you need to inspire positive powerful emotions such as desire, enthusiasm, and passion? Or, do you get action from stimulating in your audience negative emotions, such as fear and loss?

Whatever the emotion, here's the trick: Go first.

If you want to deliver a powerful emotional experience, then you must first feel it yourself. Imagine that rather than showing up at a meeting and talking about how you had to battle traffic to get there, you talk about how when you walked through the foyer, the smell of the fresh flowers reminded you of a great vacation you once took driving the countryside in Tuscany.

Starting with that emotion, what type of meeting might you have?

IT'S ABOUT SKILLS

Like the skill of skiing, the skill of communication is not this big "thing" but a series of small skills that come together. Mastering the skill of communication requires that you build up the individual skills, which you can learn from a small number of great books. Here are three examples.

1. THE BASIC SKILLS. Read Dale Carnegie's classic book *How To Win Friends and Influence People,* and you will learn many of the most important general skills of communications, such as verbal and non-verbal rapport, language, and other ideas.

2. INFLUENCE. The skills and tools of influence impact everything you do. Just mastering Robert Cialdini's six principles from his book *Influence*—reciprocity, commitment, social proof, liking, authority, and scarcity—will take you a long way.

3. PRESENTATION SKILLS. Read *The Presentation Secrets of Steve Jobs* by Carmine Gallo, and you will develop a good appreciation for what made Jobs' presentations so pleasing. Also pick up *Tell To Win* by Peter Guber, and you will learn powerful ideas for telling captivating stories and engaging your audiences.

If that were all you did, working through these books, incorporating skills over time, you would develop many of the potent skills of communication. To create experiences for people and learn the skills that make all the rest of the skills look like child's play, learn NLP and Ericksonian hypnosis.

THE PRACTICES OF COMMUNICATION

Communication is not something you think about, it is something you do, so what matters is that you practice communicating. And because you are always communicating, you too can always be practicing.

PRACTICE 1

LISTEN

Winston Churchill said, "Courage is what it takes to stand up and speak; courage is also what it takes to sit down and listen."

This is a hard one for many of us. We all like to be understood, but how many of us are excellent at first listening and understanding others?

Consider that you were given two ears and one mouth, so use them proportionately. Listen more, watch more, let people finish, and rather than opine, ask more questions. Doing this, you build rapport and have better conversations, and you also profile people so that you can enhance your communication.

PRACTICE 2

NAIL THE THREE BASICS

Many practices feed into good communication, but three of them get you much of the way by using all of the principles.

1. EYE CONTACT. When you hold someone's gaze, you engage fully in the conversation and make the other person feel that your attention is solely about him. You also can use your eyes to direct and control the person's attention. Try it: while someone's talking, look over their shoulder like you see someone you know, watch them pause and wait for you to return the attention they so crave.

2. YOUR VOICE. Read any of Obama's major speeches, and you will see that they are mostly empty words, but listen to him, and his speeches sound like words of a prophet. The secret is his voice—smooth, low, paced, and slow, like a preacher. Train your voice to be pleasing to others and commanding in tone, and you will get what you want.

3. READING NON-VERBAL LANGUAGE. In *The Definitive Book of Body Language*, Allan and Barbara Pease write, "Over 65 percent of communication is done nonverbally," and that, "in business encounters, body language accounts for between 60 and 80 percent of the impact made."

'Nuff said, right? Get excellent at reading and using non-verbal communications, and you will communicate on a completely different level.

=== PRACTICE 3 ===

PLAY CHARACTERS AND ROLES

William Shakespeare famously wrote, "All the world's a stage, and all the men and women merely players: They have their exits and their entrances; and one man in his time plays many parts, his acts being seven ages."

Think about your communication the same way: See yourself playing characters and roles. In fact, you already do this—contrast who you are with your parents versus who you are with your college mates. Now start being more deliberate, choosing the character and role you need to play for getting what you want.

For instance, imagine you are walking into a meeting with a potential client. By observing the dynamics in the room, you can determine whom you need to be in the meeting to quickly establish rapport and get that person moving to your desired outcome. At a high level, you can choose a role model of the person you need to be. Then get into the details and think about how must you walk, talk, gesture, and so on.

A note here on authenticity: No matter what characters and roles you play, you must always be authentic and true to you and your message. If you are not naturally a funny, demonstrative person, don't try to be one. Instead, think of "playing characters and roles" as either turning it up or turning it down, just like an attractive man turns up the charm when he is in a room full of ladies, and he turns up the bravado in a room full of gentlemen.

===== PRACTICE 4 =====

PRACTICE ONE PROCESS

An easy way to get good at driving the underlying process of communication is to simply choose one process to put to work in every conversation.

At a macro-level, for one whole day or week, you might practice running the same process for every meeting. For instance, if you are selling, you know in every meeting your job is to get that person interested in you and your products or services. That requires a process of building rapport, inspiring demand, clearing objections, and moving to close.

At a micro-level, you might practice just one individual process such as an agreement frame. You practice this simply by adapting your communications to find agreement with people.

It starts by finding something you can agree about, whatever the person says. Let's say that you are a Democrat speaking with a Republican who says, "Mitt Romney was robbed in the last election." You might not agree, but you can say, "You're right. He was the best Republican candidate hands down! If only he had built powerful skills of communication, he might have won!"

In this way, you aren't outright lying, but you are stimulating rapport by building agreement.

PRACTICE 5

CULTIVATE YOUR STYLE

Lyndon Johnson developed a process for building his power of personal persuasion. On his ten-point list were ideas such as: learn to remember names, practice liking people, and cultivate the quality of being interesting.

While his list is specific to him and his goals, a powerful lesson in Johnson's approach is the value in developing your own practices for cultivating your own style of communication.

Then, every chance you get, keep practicing!

CHAPTER TWENTY-ONE

THE SKILL OF SELLING

The story of the human race is the story of men and women selling themselves short.

— ABRAHAM MASLOW

★　★　★　★　★　★

The skill of selling is the most important skill of business. Period. Without an ability to sell, you have no business, and the same is true in your career.

You are always selling, both inside and outside your company. Inside, you are selling you and your ideas. Outside your company, your business is selling.

That's obvious in sales jobs, but it is also true in nearly every professional career. Every time a lawyer represents a client they are selling their next case. Each time a consultant meets with a company they are selling their next study. Even an assistant to a talent agent is selling her firm every time she talks about her boss.

Yet, although the skill of selling is crucial to almost any job or career, most people fail to train. That's partly because the notion of selling conjures up the negative imagery of a slick used car salesman, but also because, like communications, most people assume they are naturally good.

They are naturally wrong! And it costs them dearly.

The skill of selling is not just what you do when you engage with your client or customer. Selling includes everything you do in preparation for selling.

Take the standard pitch book you see for companies trying to raise capital. A boring description of the industry, boiler-plate resumes of the team, nauseating details of how the company was named and the nuances of the products or services. They have an empty swimsuit waiting for a supermodel to step inside.

But take any one of those dreary pages and bring to life the thrill of your business opportunity and how your team is going after it, and now you are selling!

Doing that requires going far beyond thinking about what you are selling so that you can understand at depth what they are buying: What matters to them? What problems do you solve for them? What opportunities do you offer? What are their objections you must overcome? How do you get them committed?

★　★　★　★　★　★

THE PRINCIPLES OF SELLING

The most important aspect of learning the skill of selling is in understanding that selling is merely a way of communicating with purpose. Hence, here you will see that these principles build on top of the skill of communication, with a bent toward integrating powerful selling devices.

BRING INTELLIGENCE

A common theme for my clients is the desire to maximize their meetings. Rather than picking up their bags and heading out the door, they have learned to step back and think carefully about what they want and then design the meeting for getting it.

Principle 1 does not require any special skills. It merely requires taking the time to prepare, think logically, determine what others want, and design strategies that lead to your desired outcome.

Sure, this takes a little time, but it takes far less than the amount of time that is typically wasted in, say, preparing the average pitch book—noodling over bullet points no one reads, pages no one sees, generic ideas no-one cares about…

Your prospect assumes you can do all the low-value work. What they are looking for is someone who has given thought to what matters to them.

======= PRINCIPLE 2 =======

SELLING IS A MINDSET, THEN
A SKILLSET

In my system of selling, there are two parts. The second part is developing your process and skills of selling. The first part is building you into the salesperson.

Clement Stone said, "Sales are contingent upon the attitude of the salesman, not the attitude of the prospect."

When you are living inside the mindset of a salesperson, you see every meeting as your opportunity to inspire a purchase. Doing this, you are not just hocking wares, or even selling yourself. You are simply walking into the room as a person of great value here to share something the other person wants.

Starting with this mindset, you stop being someone who just prepares and executes the sale. You become the sale. You bring that infectious energy, being the type of person other people want to do business with.

===== PRINCIPLE 3 =====

YOU DON'T SELL, THEY BUY!

Excellent salespeople don't focus on how they can get better at selling, they focus on getting better at helping their customers buy.

A way to think of this distinction is by separating the features from the benefits. Whereas features are about you and your product, benefits are about your client.

Master salesman Ben Feldman sold more than $1.8 billion of insurance policies in his career. Feldman said, "Don't sell life insurance. Sell what life insurance can do."

So consider the difference between saying, "We have been in business for 132 years," and saying, "Because we have been in business for 132 years, you can feel good knowing that we have exceptionally served many others like you."

One of the ways expert salespeople distinguish themselves is by seeing the world through the eyes of their clients. In marketing, this is called your avatar. Your avatar is a description of your customer, how he or she thinks, what he or she does and does not buy and why, and so on.

In becoming an expert at the skill of selling, profile the person you are selling in as much detail as possible. Learn your target's behaviors and thought patterns, and position your sale accordingly.

—— PRINCIPLE 1 ——

BUILD YOUR PROCESS

In the movie *Wall Street*, Bud Fox calls Gordon Gekko fifty-nine days in a row just to get him on the line. That's just the opening to his sale process.

If you want to master the skill of selling, you must know your entire process.

There is no such thing as a generic selling process, only the process that is built to work for you and your prospects. For instance, a top PR agent I know introduces prospects to her existing clients and gets them juiced up about working with her before discussing her fees.

While I encourage you to build your own processes for your own needs, I have two general processes for all meetings.

1. THE FIRST is a macro-selling process. That means building a process for the three steps of selling: sourcing, process, and close. Rather than running around building relationships, be clear on who you are meeting and how you sell and close.

2. THE SECOND process is a micro-process I suggest using for every meeting:

I.   INTENT: Clearly define what you want and design your meeting to get it.

II. RAPPORT: All sales happen in the context of positive rapport, so quickly and throughout the meeting, you want to build rapport.

III. PROFILING: Everything your prospect says and does gives you information on who they are and what drives them. Get good at profiling and others will think you read minds.

IV. SELL BENEFITS: Know the benefits that appeal to them and position accordingly.

V. OVERCOME OBJECTIONS: Every salesperson is accustomed to hearing the same objections over and over again (e.g., price). Know your typical objections and objection destroyers.

VI. CLOSE. The close doesn't happen at the end of the meeting. With the right intent up front, you are closing all the way through.

If you are serious about applying processes to selling, I suggest taking the previous six steps and capturing all your best ideas into a "selling black book," which you use to clearly define your process of selling. You can learn more on creating a selling black book from Tom Hopkins' excellent book, *How to Master the Art of Selling*.

===== **PRINCIPLE 5** =====

THE SKILLS OF SELLING

As with the skill of communication, the skill of selling isn't this big, mysterious "thing." It is merely a series of individual processes and skills that come together into your sale.

Here are three potent skills you can use now:

1. BUILD RELATIONSHIPS: You must forget the notion that relationships are built over time and see they are built on the underlying criteria and values that most associate with time, such as trust. If you can quickly develop these qualities, you can quickly build relationships and drive your business.

2. BEGIN WITH THE END IN MIND: For every meeting, have clear intent and be guided by your desired outcome. This skill is one of planning, foresight, and driving your agenda from beginning to end.

3. UNDERSTAND CONVERSATION FRAMES AND CONTROL: Anything you are selling is framed a certain way by you and your client. For instance, a Fortune 50 CEO might think all bankers are the same, but you can begin to frame the difference between any old banker and a trusted advisor if you tell the CEO about how Warren Buffett, who is typically critical of all bankers, came to see Goldman's Byron Trott as a person of enormous value to him.

An excellent book for learning and practicing individual skills of selling is *Unlimited Selling Power* by Donald Moine and Kenneth Lloyd. While it is a little far afield for many professional careers, the book has many powerful tools and devices you can use and practice.

★   ★   ★   ★   ★   ★

THE PRACTICES OF SELLING

Practicing the skill of selling is easy because you are always selling. Whether it's selling your kids to go to bed and your spouse on where you want to go to dinner, or inside your company, or externally with potential customers, you are constantly given the opportunity to practice the skill of selling.

As you continue practicing, not only will you continue to see how much selling is simply a way of communicating, but you will also find that positioning things in the way others want to buy them is becoming natural for you.

=== PRACTICE 1 ===

SELL TODAY

"Timid salesmen have skinny kids," noted Zig Ziglar.

Every day, find an opportunity to practice selling. Imagine you are trying to get a subordinate to quickly finish a task. You can push her, as you might have in the past, or you can practice overcoming her objections and selling the benefits of finishing quickly.

How can you sell your way past the gatekeeper to meet a CEO?

Maybe you do not yet know, but if you are trying different approaches every day, you are certain to keep deepening your skills and learning which tools work for you. Try going deep by building a personal relationship with one assistant. With another, come up with a specific "language pattern" that makes it clear how much the CEO will want to hear what you have to say.

An important part of practicing is getting good at asking for the order. On average, ninety percent of sales happen after the fifth closing attempt, so getting good at selling requires asking and asking and asking and asking and asking and asking… until you get the sale. That takes a lot of effort and conviction, but practice every day and you will soon find it easy to get what you want.

——— PRACTICE 2 ———

RUN YOUR PROCESS

Like a boxer throws a one-two combination over and over again, keep practicing your process of selling. Clearly defining your sale in your selling black book is powerful, but you build the skill through constantly running your processes.

For instance, socially or in business, when meeting someone, ask yourself: What's my intent? With your clearly defined intention, consider: *What is the process I can develop to move to my close?*

As a writer, for instance, you might be calling another writer to get her to consider promoting you. With that intent in mind, what process can you design for reaching your outcome? Can you see how that process might be the same as getting your spouse to eat at a certain restaurant? You might be profiling to understand how they think, re-iterating key benefits, flushing out and overcoming their objections, and asking for the order, over and over again.

MAKE IT FUN

Karl Marx said, "Catch a man a fish, and you can sell it to him. Teach a man to fish, and you ruin a wonderful business opportunity."

I take on few clients, but with every person I meet, my intention is to hook them into wanting what I do. Not only because I'm practicing my process, but because it is fun for me to see how I can move someone's mind from where they are to where they could be.

Most of the reasons people admonish selling have to do with being seen as slick and cheesy. But when you see that selling is just a fun way of interacting with people, where you are determining their needs and positioning what you do, all of your communications come to life.

═══ PRACTICE 4 ═══

THEM SELLING YOU

An interesting way to practice selling is to flip the script. All day every day, people are selling you. With every billboard you see, magazine you read, and conversation you have, someone is selling you something.

Practice 4 is to deconstruct how others are selling you, building deep knowledge of the skill of selling by reverse engineering, seeing what others do, and using the strategies that work.

Begin by asking: *What is their intent? Are they trying to convince me to feel validated, smart, to get something, to sell me something? And how are they selling? Are they using logic, forceful argument, emotion, authority, validating through research, etc.?*

PRACTICE SELLING ONE THING

Sitting in a selling seminar called *Persuasion Engineering*, the teacher polled the room asking: "What do you sell?" One woman sold real estate, a man sold insurance, one guy even sold services for dog grooming. Yet, after asking a number of people, the teacher turned and said:

"You are all wrong. You sell one thing: Emotion."

No matter who you are or what you are selling, you are always selling emotion. You are selling the feeling a person needs to buy from you. For each person the emotion differs, but you can be certain there are two types of emotions that stimulate all people.

The first is desire. With burning desire, a person will do what it takes to get what he wants.

The second emotion you are selling is the opposite: Fear. Ethically, of course, like an insurance salesperson builds the fear of not having insurance, get good at stimulating the fear of what they miss by not doing business with you. At the same time, practice getting good at helping others overcome the fears that are holding them back.

Remember, all communications are an experience, and selling is always an emotional journey. Watch any TV commercial, and you see that the advertisers are never selling a product, but the experience of owning it. Like showing you a mediocre car with a beautiful woman in the passenger seat, it is not the features they are selling but who the car will get you!

CHAPTER TWENTY-TWO

THE SKILL OF MINDSET

In the future, the great division will be between those who have trained themselves to handle these complexities and those who are overwhelmed by them—those who can acquire skills and discipline their minds and those who are irrevocably distracted by all the media around them and can never focus enough to learn.

— ROBERT GREENE, *MASTERY*

★　　★　　★　　★　　★　　★

In *Starting With You*, we discussed at length choosing your thinking and training your limitless mind. This topic is so important that we are covering it again, this time approaching it slightly differently.

The power tools are about impact, and because your thoughts powerfully drive your actions, the skill of mindset massively amplifies the impact you have applying the power tools.

Hence, having already extensively covered the skill of mindset, let us apply it specifically to driving the other three power tools.

★   ★   ★   ★   ★   ★

THE PRINCIPLES OF MINDSET

Remember, because the mind is a muscle you build through repetition, simply by integrating the principles into your everyday actions, you are already powerfully building your skill of mindset.

PRINCIPLE 1

MINDSET MATTERS

Your thinking is driving everything you do.

In the other three power tools, you saw references to the skill of mindset. Time management is about directing your thinking and feelings on your time. Communications and selling require clearly defining your intent and directing your actions for reaching your goal.

In all cases, your mindset guides your thinking, feelings, and actions, driving the other skills. Therefore, in applying this principle, you want to continuously remind yourself that mindset matters. Your thinking dramatically affects the way you put the other skills to work.

CHOOSING YOUR THINKING

As you learned in *Starting With You*, choosing your thinking has an enormous impact in all aspects of your career, and the same is true as it relates to applying the power tools.

For example, the hardest aspect of getting good at the skill of selling is feeling empowered to sell. It requires, among other things, getting beyond pre-conceived notions about selling, building your identity of being a salesperson, and developing the gall to ask for the order over and over again.

For many people, these examples of limited thinking hold them back, so rather than getting good at the skill of selling, they keep doing the things they have always done, getting the same results they have always gotten.

Applying this principle gives you the opportunity to choose the thoughts that drive your feelings for taking actions to develop this and other skills.

HIGHEST-VALUE THOUGHTS

Once you are choosing your thinking, why not choose your highest-value thoughts? These are the thoughts that get you taking the actions you want, and are the best thoughts you can choose.

Going back to the previous example, choosing your thinking, you might decide to say, "Give it your best shot because you've got nothing to lose." Yet, in choosing your highest-value thoughts you might amp it up again, choosing to think everyone wants what you are selling, if only you can help them understand your value proposition.

The same is true in applying all the skills. For instance, with respect to time management, is delegating hard for you because you feel you are dumping work on others? In choosing your highest-value thought, you might see the extra responsibility is exactly what they want and need to take their career to the next level.

══ PRINCIPLE 4 ══

USE ALL OF YOUR MIND

In *Starting With You*, we talked about limitless imagination. Principle 4 works the same way.

Using all of your mental resources in applying the skill of mindset, you massively enhance your impact. For example, imagine you are applying Principle 5 from the skill of time management (More Than a Feeling), and you focus on re-allocating your time from low-value tasks to a high-value task that requires deferring your gratification. While you can do this with willpower and discipline, when you use all of your mind, you have far more leverage.

Doing this, you might create a powerful visualization so that you can see how putting just ten minutes a day to that task means that in one month, you will have completed a task you otherwise would not have started. By engaging all of your mind, you are far more likely to allocate time to complete the task.

PRINCIPLE 5

THE MIND IS A MUSCLE

Even picking up a chainsaw, a lumberjack tires from chopping down trees all day. And Principle 5 reminds you that you have limited energy and will-power. Cultivating the skill of mindset enables you to have more strength and stamina in applying all of the power tools.

For instance, if you try to get fired up about selling by telling yourself that it is just something you have to do, you will tire quickly. But if you choose your thinking and select your highest-value thoughts, you will find it much easier to choose the ideas that will get you excitedly doing the things that matter to you. Not only will you willingly do more, you will do more better!

The same is true of time management. If you see time management as squeezing as much as possible into your day, it will feel hard. But if you use all of your mind and see how one more task gets you closer to your goal, you are more likely to keep powering forward.

Communication works the same way. If you think about how painful it is to get the other side to agree to a negotiation, you will likely have a long day. But if you see this constant back and forth of negotiating like a game of tennis, you change every aspect of how your day feels.

THE PRACTICES OF MINDSET

In the performance tools, we covered many cool practices for training the skill of mindset. Here I'm sharing with you specific practices my clients are currently using for driving the power tools.

THE 10-DAY CHALLENGE

For ten consecutive days, your challenge is to choose *only* your highest-value thoughts. This might be the only practice you ever need!

It's not easy to do, but the formula is straightforward. For instance, one of my CFO clients is constantly in difficult discussions with a large investor in his company. In the past, he would dread a painful back and forth before these conversations, and he would get all wound up.

In practicing the 10-Day Challenge, he approaches his conversations differently, choosing to see that even the most painful conversations are great practice for training his skill of communication.

THE FIRST RULE OF MIND CONTROL

Practicing the skill of selling can be tiresome. It's not easy to constantly hear "no," especially when you know how much your product can benefit your customer, which is the case for my client.

You will remember from earlier that the first rule of mind control is: Only think about what you want. Applying this rule, my client approaches every sale the same way, every time imagining running his sale process better, and it leading to better results.

Think about how this relates to you. What do you do that you can apply the first rule of mind control so that you keep feeling good in taking action?

REHEARSING PAST WINS

Ahead of every meeting, one of my banking clients rehearses past wins.

It is not always easy to walk into new meetings and build relationships, but by reminding himself of his past successes, my client gets the type of energy and pop he needs for approaching meetings with the right attitude.

He does this by sitting back, closing his eyes and watching mental movies of his past successes, reminding himself how quickly and easily he builds relationships.

PRACTICE 4

REHEARSING SUCCESS

In the other three power tools, you saw the importance of clearly defining your intention and directing your process and skills toward reaching your goal. In applying Practice 4, you are rehearsing having already achieved your goal.

My banking client, then, is not just looking ahead to the meeting, he is visualizing how applying the skill of communication and the skill of selling will allow him to walk out of that meeting having reached his desired outcome.

The same is true for my client who is focused on making partner. Ahead of every meeting inside and outside his firm, he visualizes how every successful meeting moves him toward making partner. By training his mind on successfully communicating and selling, he is successfully communicating and selling!

MINDSET PROGRAMMING

In *Starting With You*, you saw how your thinking drives everything you do. Here, we have covered how your thinking is specifically driving your thoughts, feelings, and actions in putting the power tools to work.

In the same way a difficult conversation for my CFO client is simply a chance for him to learn and grow his skill of communication and the same way my client has trained his mind for selling, Practice 5 is a final reminder to use every chance you get to train your thinking for taking the actions to get what you want.

CHAPTER TWENTY-THREE

WRAPPING UP
THE SYSTEM

In wrapping up *Getting Skills*, here is a quick summary of the principles and practices for each of the power tools.

Skill	Principles	Practices
TIME MANAGEMENT	1. MAKE ACTIVE CHOICES	1. DO REGULAR TIME AUDITS
	2. SHIFT YOUR TIME TO ITS HIGHEST-VALUE USE	2. PRIORITIZE IMPORTANT OVER URGENT
	3. DO WHAT YOU CHOOSE	3. USE DO AND DON'T-DO LISTS
	4. FOCUS AND CONCENTRATION	4. PLAN AHEAD
	5. MORE THAN A FEELING	5. MIND THE GAP
COMMUNICATIONS	1. IT'S ABOUT THEM	1. LISTEN
	2. AN EXPERIENCE	2. NAIL THE THREE BASIC SKILLS
	3. UNDERLYING PROCESS	3. PLAY CHARACTERS AND ROLES
	4. DRIVE STATE, DRIVE ACTIONS	4. PRACTICE ONE PROCESS
	5. IT'S ABOUT SKILLS	5. CULTIVATE YOUR STYLE
SELLING	1. BRING INTELLIGENCE	1. SELL TODAY
	2. SELLING IS A MINDSET, THEN SKILLSET	2. RUN YOUR PROCESS
	3. DON'T SELL, THEY BUY!	3. MAKE IT FUN
	4. BUILD YOUR PROCESS	4. THEM SELLING YOU
	5. THE SKILLS OF SELLING	5. PRACTICE SELLING ONE THING
MINDSET	1. MINDSET MATTERS	1. THE 10-DAY CHALLENGE
	2. CHOOSING YOUR THINKING	2. THE FIRST RULE OF MIND CONTROL
	3. HIGHEST-VALUE THOUGHTS	3. REHEARSING PAST WINS
	4. USE ALL OF YOUR MIND	4. REHEARSING SUCCESS
	5. THE MIND IS A MUSCLE	5. MINDSET PROGRAMMING

FINISHING THE SYSTEM

This brings us to the end of *The System*. So, before moving on, let's do a quick review of what we have covered in the most advanced system ever built for doing what you want in your career.

STEP 5

GETTING SKILLS

We just made our way through *Getting Skills,* which is sequentially the final step but, like a street and its lights run parallel, is a step you have been taking throughout this guide.

STEP 4

EXECUTE IT

We went through the most important ideas in putting to work your plan, taking the action steps toward getting what you want.

STEP 3

PLAN IT

Before getting to *Execute It,* we covered *Plan It*, where you took the ideas from steps 1 and 2 and developed your plan. You will remember that we also discussed that rather than seeing *Plan It* and *Execute It* as separate steps, it is important to see your plan as an iterative process, continuously planning and executing toward what you want.

STEP 2

GETTING IT

The most important step we took was *Getting It,* where you went deep into your career and developed the intelligence behind *Your System.* Here, you not only focused on cracking the code of your career, but also on working through the models, principles, and strategies to build your strategy, competitive advantage, and brand.

STEP 1

DEFINE IT

We began with *Define It.* Here, not only did you figure out what you want, you began building your process for getting it.

Putting all those pieces together, what you see is that we have taken your career and broken it down in such a way that you have built and are putting to work *Your System for Doing What You Want!*

PART 3:

SCHEMING AND

DREAMING

CHAPTER TWENTY-FOUR

GETTING PAID AND PROMOTED

If you are good at something, never do it for free!

— THE JOKER, *THE DARK KNIGHT*

★ ★ ★ ★ ★ ★

I know a rock star investment banker at Goldman Sachs.

Since the day he joined as an associate out of business school, he has stood out. He is not just a top performer; he is truly exceptional. If you met this guy, within a minute you would know he takes his career seriously and does everything he can to serve his clients and deliver value to the firm.

He has worked on some of the firm's most important deals and accounts and has taken on roles with increasing responsibility. He is a great team player and incredibly loyal. Even as a managing director, he works as hard as an analyst: in the office until midnight, weekends, work-filled vacations.

You get the point: You would struggle to find anyone more dedicated. He gives it his all. He even relocated his family to Europe to build his platform for partner.

So, two years ago when he was up for partner, it wasn't as though he was a shoe-in, it was a tough year for promotion, yet even still, he's exactly the type of banker you'd expect to make it.

But when the list came out, his name was left off. You would be shocked...

If you hadn't seen it many times over.

We've all seen it.

And it's not as if these superstars who live and breathe their work don't "deserve" promotion. But getting promoted doesn't work that way.

Put yourself in the shoes of his bosses and it is easy to see why you too might look past the rock star managing director. A good soldier is great at taking orders, jumping on grenades, and storming hills, but those are rarely the characteristics you want in your partner. He will also work even harder to make partner in future years. So why in the world would you promote him?

What's the cost versus benefit for the firm and you personally? The only cost is that he will be disappointed, but the firm doesn't lose anything. A good soldier is someone who will only work harder for your approval.

And that is why many like him keep getting passed over, year after year. Working hard and being exceptional isn't good enough. To keep getting paid and promoted, you must be doing more.

A DELIBERATE APPROACH

In my private client work, I strive to deliver ten times my fee in tangible dollar value. I call this a 10X Guarantee. Irrespective of the intangible benefits of transforming my clients' careers and lives, we are always focused on driving two sources of dollar value—getting paid and promoted.

This guide is built to work the same way.

While everything you have already learned should certainly result in you getting paid more and promoted faster, in this section I am sharing with you advanced approaches specifically built for getting paid and promoted.

These ideas are not for all of you. For some of you, getting paid and promoted is straightforward, such as my friend Molly, an executive in an advertising agency who gets paid according to the revenues she generates. For some of you, there is little more you can or need to do. But in other careers, where getting paid and promoted depends on a subjective set of factors, there might be many different things you can do.

THE OPPORTUNITY

Over the years, I have talked to many people about managing their compensation and promotion processes. Interestingly, many of the most successful people I know rarely think about it. They have found that by doing a great job, their company looks after them.

While this passive approach works for some, it patently fails many others.

During the credit crisis, one of my former bosses, who had always been looked after by the firm, found himself in a position where his business evaporated overnight.

So did his promotion track. A good team player, he had believed that he would be at the firm for the long-run, so during the credit boom, he had failed to maximize his opportunity, not only turning down far more lucrative jobs but also failing to maximize his compensation year-to-year.

Your company is a rational economic animal. In the good years, it will pay you what it needs to keep you motivated and loyal. If your business slows down and your value is diminished, you will be a resource that, like gold, quickly loses value.

So it's up to you. You can sit back and let someone else determine your value, or you can take responsibility for getting paid and promoted.

IT'S UP TO YOU

When I was a vice president at Goldman Sachs, I remember watching a managing director in his compensation discussion with the partner who ran the office.

When the meeting began, they were just rapping. It looked casual and easy, but I could feel an obvious tension in the room. When the partner started speaking in his all-business tone, I could see the managing director getting more and more serious. His body stiffened. His face grew more tense. He obviously wasn't happy.

As the conversation went back and forth, I could see the managing director getting increasingly frustrated. Then, like a worn-out fan belt, he snapped. He raised his voice, threw his notepad across the room, and stormed out.

The next day, he was back at his desk. The frustration had worn off. He crept around the office sheepishly.

He would stick around, and his career would remain stagnant because he had turned himself into a helpless victim who responds to conflict by throwing tantrums.

Do you know how many times I have heard people say things like, "I got screwed on compensation!"

If that ever comes out of your mouth, I have news for you: You are wrong.

If you do not get what you want, then it is up to you to figure out how to do better. And if year after year, you are being treated "unfairly," but you continue to stick around, then clearly your company is pricing you correctly: They are paying you exactly what they need so that you keep supplying your labor.

If you think you are getting treated unfairly, don't throw a hissy fit and keep showing up. Instead take the sage advice of Motley Crue: "Don't go away mad, girl. Just go away."

In your career, taking responsibly requires active career management and a deliberate approach. That begins with taking responsibly for the one thing that matters most.

* * * * * *

WHAT MATTERS MOST?

If you ask a bunch of people what one thing matters most in getting paid and promoted in their career, you will likely hear a range of different answers.

Yet, no matter what the career or answer you hear, they all come back to just one thing that matters most.

Here it is: The one thing that matters most in getting paid and promoted...

Value. Value, value, value, value, value.

I said it before, and I will say it again: If you don't remember everything else, remember value. Of all the things that matter in doing what you want in your career, what matters most is that you are a creator of value.

LeBron doesn't get paid for lacing up and hitting the court. He gets paid for the value he brings to the team. Your job works the same.

When you realize that value is *the* driver of doing what you want, you begin to see that every other driver of success in your career is merely one source of value.

* * * * * *

WHAT GOT YOU HERE WON'T GET

YOU THERE

It is reasonable to expect that if you want to keep getting paid more and promoted, you must keep delivering more value. Delivering more value means knowing how to keep mining more of your sources of value and delivering more gold. It also means understanding how your sources of value change over time.

I met with a recently promoted partner from a private equity fund. He told me he felt good about his formula for success which had gotten him to partner but he also knew the game had changed.

"What I have done has worked well in the past, but I know that what got me here won't get me there."

He had stolen my line, which is the title of one of my favorite books by leading executive coach, Marshall Goldsmith.

Ralph Waldo Emerson once said, "Big jobs usually go to the men who prove their ability to outgrow small ones." While proving your mettle in your previous role got you to where you are, now you need to know what is required to get you to your next role.

My friend realized that becoming a successful partner required building an entirely different platform for his career. However he looked at it, he saw he was now being valued differently inside his firm, and it wasn't just a matter of driving more value. Now he had to drive the right type of value.

Not only do you want to have a firm understanding of what drives your value, but you also want to know how your sources of value must change over time. That's the first part to getting paid and promoted—knowing how you keep driving the right type of value.

The second part is the focus of the next chapter.

CHAPTER TWENTY-FIVE

BROADCASTING YOUR VALUE

Without promotion, something terrible happens... nothing!

— P.T. BARNUM

★　　★　　★　　★　　★　　★

I heard a story that trickled down from a senior executive who worked closely with Steve Jobs. This executive was once asked what Steve Jobs perceived to be a powerful secret of success. The answer was something like: "Take what you do well and broadcast it on as big of a canvas as possible."

Steve Jobs wasn't just a visionary creator of tools that transformed our lives. He was a genius at packaging, marketing, and advertising his products. He was far beyond a creator of great value; he was a man who knew how to share his value with the world.

In getting paid and promoted, the same is required of you. Just as Steve Jobs could have invented a great technology and waited for the world to discover him, you can take a passive approach and hope your bosses and firm recognize you for all the value you are creating. Or you can take an active approach, ensuring your bosses and firm know what value you are creating. I call this broadcasting your value.

And let's be honest: Few of us are comfortable being self-promoters. Most of us are modest-types who hope others recognize all the good things we do. But the fact is, if you are not broadcasting your own success, then likely nobody is.

YOU DOWN WITH MPC?

However you look at it, broadcasting your value is about influence. It is about getting in front of the right people and helping them see things your way. The MPC framework is a simplified version of a more thorough model I use for teaching selling and influence.

If influencing others is important to getting paid and promoted, this framework will benefit you. It can also be used for any purposes (selling, landing a job, even quitting your job) where influencing others matters to getting what you want.

The MPC framework stands for Meet, Process, Close.

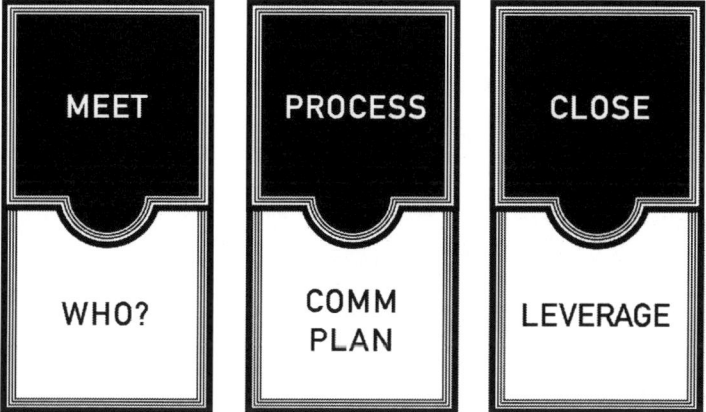

First, define who you need to influence. Second, develop your process of influence. Finally, move to close, which means going from engaging your targets to getting your desired outcome.

Before we get started, I want to point out two aspects of putting the MPC framework to work. First, as a framework for influence, it is only as good as your skills of communication, influence, and selling. To use this approach effectively, apply the principles and practice your skills.

Second, use the MPC Framework with the right intent and frame of mind. Consider the wrong frame of mind akin to the problem some people have in networking. Seeing every person as a "network node," they fail to see that networking is about enjoying people and giving them a reason to want to spend time with you.

Applying the MPC framework for getting paid and promoted works the same way.

Nobody likes the schemer who tries to get what he wants through manipulation and subversion. Use this framework authentically—to genuinely connect with people and give them reasons to support you and your success. Yes, you can be calculating and strategic, but be subtle, understated, and ethical. This way, everyone will want you to succeed.

═══ STEP 1 ═══

MEET

"Meet" means: Whom do you need to influence?

Depending on your job and what drives you in getting paid and promoted, this might be a short or a long list of people inside and outside your firm.

In many jobs, this is a short list of people who are directly responsible for your fate. But, in other jobs, such as that of a politician, where every vote counts, you want to be kissing a lot of babies. Even in cases where you only require the support of your direct bosses, I suggest you more broadly seek the support of other senior decision-makers. This is particularly important at more senior levels, where promotions can be the result of some form of internal cross-referencing process. In these cases, you might draw a broad circle for meeting and influencing key people inside your company.

Also consider that in some jobs you derive great value by references that come externally from your clients and others. A friend in management consulting estimates that a glowing email from a client is worth five times what anyone inside his firm might say about him.

Once you have created your list for "meet," you also want to begin thinking carefully about the right ways of approaching each person. Profile them to an extreme. Figure out in detail what they respond to, and design a tailored process for influencing each person.

═══ STEP 2 ═══

PROCESS

In Step 2, you develop a rigorous approach to communicating your message to each and every person you meet.

While many people approach compensation and promotion discussions lightly, the better way is to approach these meetings as you would any important and complex sale—by clearly defining how you sell yourself and your requests.

Before we discuss formulating your communication plan, let me share an example of how this can come together.

Go for win-win!

One of my favorite books on negotiation is *Getting To Yes*, which is not only an exemplary book on negotiation, but also provides a potent contrast on how *not* to negotiate.

Sadly, even today, too few people follow this approach. Too often, we find ourselves caught in what is called positional bargaining. Like our so-called leaders in government who are unable to agree on anything, we pit our interests against another person or group's interest.

Then we grind each other down, eventually getting to an outcome with which neither side is happy. In its essence, positional bargaining is the awful philosophy that a successful negotiation is one in which neither party feels he or she got their desired outcome. Unfortunately, this lose-lose model of negotiation not only sets up a conflict of relationship and substance, but it also leads to suboptimal outcomes.

A better approach of negotiating your compensation and promotion is to go for a win-win, mutually-beneficial outcome. Rather than trading off against each other, instead focus on a higher mutually beneficial intention, and design a structure for the negotiation that enables you and your bosses to get your desired outcome. In the win-lose model, this is structurally impossible. In the win-win model, having both parties feel good is the intent.

For six to eight weeks, one of my clients and I focused on developing his communication strategy for his compensation discussion. We also tailored the message specifically for his bosses—without their knowledge, of course! His bosses went into the compensation discussion with no idea that we had laid out the entire board. They were prepared to engage in a grind-him-down fight, but instead, my client merely reminded them of all the things of value that matter to them. For him to keep digging deeper and creating more value, he explained that he wanted to be compensated a certain way.

Rather than implying, "This is what I want; give it to me," he implied, "This is what we all want, and this is how we get there." In this way, he wasn't pushing a problem for them to solve, but a solution so that everyone got more of what they want. Beyond that, we also built an extremely potent device into the negotiation by the way we anchored the entire discussion. Rather than anchoring on his market value or the details of his cash and non-cash compensation, instead, we picked an emotional rationale they couldn't help but buy into.

My client got the eight-figure package he wanted, and his bosses felt great about giving it to him. That type of win-win was only possible because he approached the discussion by seeing the world through his bosses' eyes. He positioned his discussion in terms of what they value. That was possible because he spent an inordinate amount of time preparing his communication plan.

YOUR COMMUNICATION PLAN

There is no better way of getting paid and promoted than taking the time to create a thoughtful approach for communicating your message. While it does require some effort up front, it will easily pay off in your results.

As Napoleon Hill said, "The man who does more than he is paid for will soon be paid for more than he does."

Of course, you will only be willing to create this plan if you are serious about getting what you want. So the first step of developing your communication plan is to own it.

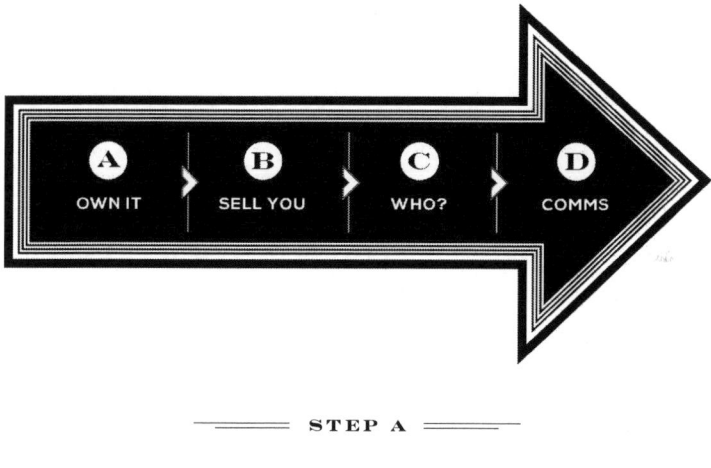

STEP A

OWN IT

If you only kinda, perhaps, maybe wanna get paid and promoted, then don't bother. You will fail.

People who do not own the responsibility for getting paid and promoted hold back and say things like, "Well, let's see how it goes."

DO WHAT YOU WANT

They think: *They better take care of me this year.*

But getting paid and promoted requires you to set the intention and take the actions to make it happen. That's not easy to do. It requires going after it and doing hard things, having potentially difficult conversations, and knowing you might fail. But when you own it and ask for the order, you also open the door to succeeding.

As you saw earlier, a powerful rule of selling is that you must not only ask for the order, but you must keep asking and asking. On average, ninety percent of sales happen after the fifth closing attempt, which means the salesperson who remains hungry and aggressive and keeps doing what is hard—asking for the order—is more likely to succeed.

This does not mean you want to be overt about your request and your demands! In some cases, you can be straightforward, and you will be best served by communicating your request clearly and firmly. But depending on the person, the custom, culture, or any number of factors, you might instead seed ideas or otherwise ask for the order covertly. In any case, you can frame your ask in a way that will be well received.

Imagine sitting down with your boss at the start of the promotion year and saying, "Look, it is important to me that I get promoted this year. I know everything I have done in the past has me well positioned, and it is up to me to earn my promotion by creating more value for the company. And it is important to me that by continuing to deliver, I am considered this year."

Then you go on, "This is important to me, so I would like to ensure that over the course of the year, we keep discussing whether I am on track for promotion. Please be honest with me. If there are more things I can be doing, please let me know. Getting promoted is important to me and how I think about continuing to deliver value to the company."

Here, you own your goal, over-communicate its importance, and take responsibility for creating the value to justify your promotion. Also, of course, you are giving a slight indication of how this might affect the way you think about performing your role. There are many ways you can communicate your message, yet what matters is that you are taking responsibility and owning it.

───── STEP B ─────

SELL YOU FIRST, THEN THEM

To build the persuasive arguments in your communication plan, step back and think about what you would need to hear if you were in your bosses' shoes. Then, before you sit with those on your "meet" list, practice convincing five of your trusted advisors.

Your communication plan should be created only after you have considered a few questions:

• WOULD YOU PAY and promote you? Why? Why not?

• WHAT WOULD YOU NEED to hear from you to justify a promotion?

• WHAT'S SO COMPELLING in your case relative to others in your position?

Really grill yourself here because if you cannot convince yourself, then you sure as hell should not expect to convince others. But when you can easily convince yourself and your advisors, you have built a compelling case.

In crafting your ideas, think about these three categories:

1. SELLING POINTS: What are the arguments in your favor? Like you would for selling a house, create detailed selling points that justify

your ask. And remember: Do not create a list of what you think are your key selling points. Create a list through the eyes of your bosses. How do they value you?

2. OBJECTIONS: Carefully consider why they might object to your ask. Where have you failed? What are your weaknesses? Where do others outperform you? Then, come up with the mitigating responses and objection destroyers. Ideally, your communication plan should destroy objections before anyone has a chance to raise them.

3. REMEMBER: This is selling, baby! It's not just a matter of having all the right points but rather of selling in a way that is convincing.

If you want to get paid and promoted, not only do you need to develop all the right ideas, but you must be able to present those ideas in a way that is compelling to others. To do this, I suggest building your communication plan like the selling black book I mentioned in the skill of selling. Develop a rigorous approach to selling your greatest asset!

STEP C

WHO?

In *How To Win Friends and Influence People*, Dale Carnegie tells a story of a man who, after attending Carnegie's seminar, learned to influence his child. Coming home one night, he found his youngest son lying on the floor having a tantrum because he did not want to attend the first day of kindergarten the following day. Whereas in the past he would reprimand the boy, he tried a different approach.

He thought: *What would be exciting about going to kindergarten?* Then, he and his wife began finger-painting on the kitchen table. When the boy naturally came over to enjoy the fun, the father told him that he would get to enjoy more of this tomorrow at kindergarten. Of course, the boy became excited about attending.

This second rule of influence is summed up by Carnegie's famous phrase, "Arouse in the other person an eager want."

In the principle of Step C, this means that your communication plan is not about what you want but about arousing in your bosses a desire to deliver what you want. So, what is the reason each of your targets will be eager to deliver what you want?

This requires some level of "profiling" each person. Ask yourself:

- *How do they think?*

- *WHAT has their career been like?*

- *WHAT do they value?*

- *WHAT do they value in me specifically?*

- *How do I appeal to them? Influence them?*

Asking these types of questions will give you a lot of intelligence for positioning your discussions, and you can go a step further too.

I recently pointed out to my client a subtle difference in the communication styles of two leaders in his company. In emails, one of them uses process words like "doing" and the other uses outcome words like "done." By profiling your targets and noticing details like this, you are able to tell what people value. In this case, one values progress and the other values completion.

Modeling each person you meet enables you to frame all of your conversations based on what that person specifically values. You must know who you are communicating with and tailor your message accordingly. And remember: There is no such thing as generic selling or communication.

Finally, in this step—"who?"—you also identify the people you are competing against. The candid truth is: When your bosses pay and promote you, they will likely hold back someone else. So it is your job to know who you are competing against and how you outcompete them. Ask:

- *How would my bosses justify it to my competitors?*

- *How would my bosses justify it to themselves?*

- *Do I want to blow them out or play nice?*

- *What are my competitors doing to compete against me?*

===== STEP D =====

COMMUNICATE

The final step to your communication plan is action-oriented. It's going beyond planning to actually communicating.

This is typically the hardest step, but if you have done your preparation right, and you have practiced, you might actually find this step the easiest. This is because you have taken a rigorous and in-depth approach, whereas most meetings will be ridiculously shallow.

When I was applying for jobs as an investor, I first spent one thousand hours developing a selling black book that included all the questions and answers I expected. I had clearly over-prepared. Only a fraction of the questions in my selling black book were asked, but almost all of the questions that were asked were in my book. Having researched and profiled each person, determined what they valued, and told them what they wanted to hear, the interviews were decidedly easy.

Important to this step is determining how you choose to communicate. In some cases, you might decide to set up formal meetings and communicate overtly, whereas in other cases you might communicate more subtly over time, potentially even covertly. The difference can be characterized as leading versus seeding.

When you ask directly, you are leading. You are setting the agenda and asking for the order, leading the other person to your desired outcome. Here's a six-step process for a leading conversation.

1. THE PERSON'S STATE: Remember the rules of selling and communication. Begin by getting your target into an emotional state which promotes a productive conversation. Any topic that gets the person smiling and nodding does the trick.

2. SET UP YOUR ASK: Emphasize how important it is to you. Talk about the value you have created and how you justify your ask. Get the person bought into your frame, your anchor, and the logical sequence which leads to your ask.

3. ASK FOR THE ORDER: Having clearly led to how you got to your ask, lay it out there. Ask for what you want, reinforce how important it is to you and how you arrived at this view from your logical process.

4. CLEAR OBJECTIONS: Think carefully about what the person's objections might be and be ready to counter. For example, the person might say: "I will get push-back from others," and you might respond, "What would you need to do to get them on side?" Your job is not done until you have cleared all their objections and have them on board!

5. ISSUE A CHALLENGE: Give the person an opportunity to rise to a challenge for you. For instance, you might say, "Look, I understand, the company just might not be flexible enough." Or give the person a way to prove his or her power by saying something like, "I recognize there are other powerful decision-makers you need to convince."

6. CLEARLY DEFINE WHAT HAPPENS NEXT: Take responsibility for following up on anything else you need to do. Reinforce the importance of your ask, and cycle back to step 1 by closing in a positive state.

In seeding ideas, you operate far more subtly, dropping ideas (potentially over a number of months) that enable your targets to believe they reached their own conclusion.

For instance, rather than walking into your boss' office and laying down the law on how you must get promoted this year, tell her random stories that have a similar structure, knowing that at some level, she is getting the point. An overt approach is to talk about how someone else got promoted at some other company, of course implying that you expect the same. But a more advanced covert approach might be to talk about a different topic entirely, such as how your plumber requested you promote him to ten of your friends but you refused, so he did not do the job, and now it is a hassle and you need to find someone else!

Now that might sound too circuitous, but done right, seeding ideas is far more powerful because even though you are planting the seeds, you are allowing the other people to think they reached their own conclusion. When you are communicating expertly, using tools others don't know exist, you are far more likely to get what you want.

Okay. That's it for steps A-D of your communication plan, which is the second step of the MPC framework. We covered a lot in this step and to ensure you are integrating these important ideas, I suggest you go back and do a quick review before you move to the third step of the MPC framework.

═══ STEP 3 ═══

CLOSE

Step 3 is about leverage. It requires firmly answering your target's most vulnerable question: "What if we don't promote you?" That often means adding teeth.

A couple of years ago, I got a call from a former colleague as I was driving the I-70 toward Denver. I was living in Vail skiing for the season, and I had not spoken to this former colleague in some time. He was calling to tell me that after thirteen-plus years, he had just resigned.

He went on to say, "You know, I'm not like you. I was loyal, I did what was asked of me, and they did not take care of me."

I burst out laughing.

Here's why: Loyalty, schmoyalty. I have been loyal to every *person* who has been loyal to me, but there is no such thing as *company* loyalty.

My world collapsed when I learned that half of my colleagues were let go after the Internet bubble burst in 2000. And my heart broke again when almost all of my former leveraged finance colleagues were let go after the credit bubble burst in 2008. That does not make the firm "bad." Remember: your company is just a rational economic animal that rewards value not loyalty.

This means if you want to get your company to give you more value, you must think as it thinks. If you are trying to get paid more or promoted faster because you have "earned," "deserve," or otherwise think you are owed it, think again. Your company cares little. And it is unlikely to do anything beyond what it needs to keep getting what it wants from you.

So why should you think differently?

WHAT IS GOOD LEVERAGE?

Without a good answer for your company's question—"What if we don't pay and promote you?"—you are unlikely to keep aggressively getting paid and promoted. So what's a good answer?

You of course know that leverage is crucial in any exchange of value. If the dealer has ten identical cars gathering dust on the lot you will get a better deal. The same is true in getting paid and promoted. In this sense, your most evident source of leverage is another job offer, but it's also an obvious and dangerous card to play.

Many marriages and careers alike have ended because of bad communications. Often someone using an alternative job offer doesn't actually want to leave, but is instead trying to get more love from their current employer. Yet, presented badly, they often only harm their career.

In some cases, another job offer can work in your favor. If you get another offer from a place your company respects, and you have support inside your company, you might get your bosses' competitive juices flowing and spark a bidding war for you.

But in most cases, particularly in a company that values teamwork and loyalty and where you have insufficient power, playing the bid-away card will likely backfire. Your bosses might turn against you, and you will be left playing your card for the final time.

Remember, this is delicate business. As Marvin Levin put it: "If you are planning on doing business with someone again, don't be too tough in the negotiations. If you're going to skin a cat, don't keep it as a house cat."

No one wants to fight for a mercenary. And ultimatums often backfire because they are typically the hand played by someone with a weak negotiating position. Like a kid in the schoolyard threatening to take his ball and run away, any person of power knows that threatening with another offer is often the only alternative for someone unable to step up and play the damn game.

So only play this hand if you are willing to walk, and if you think you can manage your discussions so that they work to your advantage. To do that, be extremely deliberate in your discussions, ensuring you are thoughtfully and respectfully positioning your alternative offer inside your company. You might do this by saying something like: "I really want to stay here. I imagined being here the rest of my career, but what they are offering me is just too good to turn down."

Ensure that you have thought through all of the back-and-forth before having your conversations. In adding leverage to getting paid and promoted, you might also explore other subtle forms of influence.

Imagine that throughout the year and with every chance you get, you simply keep talking about how enamored you are with certain CEOs and entrepreneurs. You talk about the meetings you have had with impressive leaders, books you have read, and how many other exciting things are going on in the world. Paired with exceptional performance and all the qualities of being a long-term "franchise" player, you send a signal that suggests the onus is on your company to keep convincing you that this is the right long-term play.

Of course, these are just two examples of varying degrees of influence, and hopefully you are seeing that there is a plethora of overt and covert strategies you can use for gaining leverage.

The greatest leverage you have is in using the type of leverage winners use. That is the type of leverage that comes from everyone knowing you are the type of player who has other options. You don't need a specific approach to doing this. You don't need to position and posture yourself. When you are the type of person your company must work to retain, it's obvious—unsaid.

Rather than going out of your way to prove to everyone you are a loyal schmo, instead make it clear that you love your company for the opportunities they have given you, implying you could love another company that offered you the right opportunities too! In this way, you are playing The Company Man—The Company Man with plenty of options.

Remember: This isn't just leverage you develop and use "against" your boss; you develop leverage "for" your boss. Getting you paid and promoted is often about your boss having to negotiate the system, so your closing strategies are also arming your boss to fight for you.

SQUEAKY WHEEL

When advocating on compensation and promotion, few of us want to be perceived as the squeaky wheel. Even though you know the squeaky wheel gets the grease, few people want to make a fuss on these topics, particularly in this market. Right?

No one wants to be that guy who is always whining about how he got paid. Or the woman all year talking about how if she doesn't get promoted, she is gonna do this or that. No one wants to be around them, let alone be them.

Putting this approach to work, you never have your discussions in the squeaky-wheel way. Instead, deliver more of the right value to your firm and focus on win-win outcomes, then carefully craft your communication in an empowering way.

In *Negotiation*, author Michael Schatzki cites a hiring manager who negotiates hard on salary and terms with employees who have just been hired.

Schatzki says that many people feel sheepish when trying to negotiate salary in their future jobs because they worry it will muddy their relationships before they get started.

This hiring manager said just the opposite. Schatzki asked her, "So you don't get annoyed or think of people as ingrates when they negotiate with you?"

"Not at all," she said. "On the contrary, it indicates a self-assurance and confidence that I value very highly in my employees."

CHAPTER TWENTY-SIX

MANIPULATING PERCEPTION

Perception is projection.

— CARL JUNG

★   ★   ★   ★   ★   ★

H aving now covered a detailed framework for planning and executing your compensation and promotion discussions, let us cover a more indirect approach—strategies for managing your company review process.

Again, these ideas are not right for all of you. While many companies have an internal review process, these ideas might not be right for you in your career. Yet, even if that's the case, I suspect you will find these ideas helpful in framing discussions in your career.

While your reviews are strangely considered objective feedback, they are of course highly subjective. And therefore, with the right strategy, you can meaningfully influence your reviews, and the most "objective" measure of how you are perceived and rewarded.

Here are five strategies for managing your company's review process.

STRATEGY 1

USE INFORMAL REVIEWS

Remember, feedback is absolutely essential to optimizing your performance. However, you want to ensure the feedback you collect is not working to your detriment but to your benefit.

So, rather than waiting for feedback in your formal reviews, instead, throughout the year seek informal feedback, which you can use to improve your performance and also feed-forward your success (as we discussed in *Getting It*) into your formal reviews.

The value of your informal feedback is only as good as the questions you ask. Rather than asking general questions about your performance, instead, put together a list of powerful questions that stimulate the type of feedback that enables you to take action.

For instance, rather than asking: *How am I doing relative to my peers? Instead ask: What are the best people doing that I am not doing?* And really drill down into what more you can be doing to not just excel at your current level, but to powerfully drive your career forward.

STRATEGY 2

GENERAL PERCEPTION

Perception is projection and how you project yourself creates the entire perception of your performance. This means that if you want outstanding reviews, you want to deliver and project outstanding performance. But you do this in more subtle ways too.

For instance, in keeping senior people abreast of what you are doing and getting them involved where appropriate, you are feeding forward to those who may only get limited direct exposure to you.

This same idea applies to every interaction in your company. For instance, when you run into people in your office, the attitude you present and the way you talk about your business completely forms their perception of you. When these people run into your boss, they might say something like, "It seems so-and-so is really crushing it." That one line goes a long way in driving your perception.

The same, of course, applies to the way you interact every day with those around you. Everyone you interact with drives the perception of who you are and the job you are doing, and in ways you can never underestimate might appear in your reviews.

To massively impact your reviews, strategize and use your everyday office chatter. Project your best and create that perception of you.

STRATEGY 3

MANAGE YOUR REVIEWERS

The quality of your reviews is not determined just by what is written, but also by who writes it. Not only do different colleagues carry more heft in the organization, but each also has a different approach to writing reviews. If appropriate, be thoughtful about how you manage each of your reviewers.

For instance, if you know a certain colleague is overly complimentary and will strongly support you in your reviews, find more opportunities to work with them and give them more ways to keep supporting you. Similarly, if you work with someone who is overly critical, consider working less with them, or excessively feeding-forward and giving them chances to provide you with informal feedback.

STRATEGY 4

PRIMACY AND RECENCY

A notion in psychology, primacy and recency means that us humans are more likely to remember things that occur at the beginning and the end.

So applying this principle to your reviews, you might seek to start your year with a bang, impressing the heck out of people, then chill a little more throughout the year, then pick up your performance in the couple of months right before the review process begins.

It's sneaky. It works. Use it.

STRATEGY 5

SELF REVIEW

The final strategy is managing your self-review.

The self-review is not for you to track or assess your own performance. The self-review is so that your reviewers know how you assess your own performance. The most important aspect of the self-review is self-awareness, demonstrating consistency relative to what others write of you.

In this regard, you are much more advantaged in failing to highlight one of your strengths than you are at missing one of your weaknesses. The self-review can also be a useful tool in destroying objections, negating your weaknesses by providing supporting thoughts in regard to weaknesses you expect others to highlight in your reviews. In the same way objection-destroyers work in selling, concerns that you can blow out on your own will stick less.

For instance, imagine you are a senior consultant who has underperformed at bringing in business. In your self-review, you might highlight how you wish you had brought in more business this year, but also how much you focused on building long-term relationships that you expect to keep paying off over time.

CHAPTER TWENTY-SEVEN

GETTING OUT

For the past 33 years, I have looked in the mirror every morning and asked myself: 'If today were the last day of my life, would I want to do what I am about to do today?' And whenever the answer has been 'No' for too many days in a row, I know I need to change something.

— STEVE JOBS

★　★　★　★　★　★

Michael Cavanagh was a J.P. Morgan lifer.

At least, that is what everyone thought of the co-head of investment banking after he dedicated fourteen years of service to the firm.

Then, shockingly, in March 2014 he resigned to take the role of co-COO of the Carlyle Group.

The rumor mill swirled. Why would the man potentially in line for the top job resign? Was it due to the increased regulatory scrutiny and heightened banking competition? Was it something he learned during the investigation into the "London Whale" trading loss that cost the firm $20 billion?

All interesting theories, yet perhaps the most telling answer is from Cavanagh himself.

"I just decided to take a different turn in my career," he said. A year later he took a different turn again, resigning from Carlyle to become the CFO of Comcast.

Although it is less common for someone of Cavanagh's seniority and position to up and leave, almost everyone in a professional career is sometimes, if not always, thinking about getting out of their current job.

There is no longer such thing as a job for life, and even those of us who joined our jobs expecting to be there for the rest of our careers often find ourselves questioning the path.

For some of us, it begins nearly the moment we get settled. After years of thinking ahead to what it will be like, we're often surprised. As my friend who left his first job in strategic planning at Disney after only nine months in the job said, "It wasn't what I had imagined it would be."

Soon after getting started many of us are thinking ahead to our next move. Do you go to graduate school? Do you make a move inside your company? Do you do something different?

From that point forward, for many of us it is much the same thing. As you get more senior, you become more entrenched, but also the stakes keep rising.

You're asking yourself, do you want to be there for the rest of your career? Is this what you expected your career and life to be?

All the way from the bottom to the top, many of us are constantly evaluating our options for getting out. And, although our alternatives differ wildly, our goal is the same:

How do you keep evaluating your options and making the right moves for doing what you want?

BEGGING FOR CHANGE

How many people do you know who want to make a change in their career?

Likely quite a few. You might even be one of them. Yet of all the people you know who talk about changing jobs, leaving their company, or perhaps even starting something of their own, how many do it?

Reflect on that for a moment. Of all the people you know, how many have made the career moves they would like to make?

It is easy to dream of walking into your boss' office and handing in your notice.

It is easy to dream of imagining yourself sitting in a different job.

It is easy to dream of chasing that ideal career you can imagine.

It is easy to dream.

Yet few people ever wake up and do it.

Many people know that they do not want to be in their current job forever, but with different options to consider, little time, and lacking a sophisticated approach, few people ever do what is required for making good moves.

Lacking clear direction for what they want, many find themselves simply reacting to the opportunities around them. If they happen to get a call from a headhunter or someone offers to introduce them to another opportunity, they might consider making a move.

But like the club girl who waits until 2 a.m. to meet Mr. Right-now, they are hardly maximizing their options.

Worse yet, many people only seriously consider making moves when they are pushed, which of course is the worst time to jump.

Of the many people who were laid-off after the Internet bubble burst in 2000 when I was based in Menlo Park, the ones who were thinking ahead, knew their BATNA, and had a back-up plan quickly got back to work. Others were unemployed for years.

Thinking ahead for reacting to change is important, but in creating the career you truly want, you need to go one massive step further by developing a sophisticated approach for proactively *driving* change.

That requires two things: First, a way of framing your choices for evaluating your options and directing your career; and second, strategies for making the right choices in navigating your career. While this is not easy to do, in *Getting Out,* we make it much, much easier for you.

*   *   *   *   *   *

BACK TO THE DUAL-TRACK

Richer than Warren Buffett, the third richest man on the planet, retailer Amancio Ortega, once said, "We cannot limit ourselves to continuing on the path we have already opened."

I suggest that you follow his advice, so let's revisit your roadmap, as we left off back in *Define It*. Having covered in detail the status-quo track of executing in your current career, let us now explore your alternative tracks.

Your roadmap gives you a way of conceptualizing the many career tracks available to you. So rather than simply focusing on the career track out ahead of you to the exclusion of other options, it gives you a way of mapping the many options that keep you moving toward your grandest vision. Putting to work your roadmap, therefore, you constantly evaluate the merits of staying on your status-quo track relative to your alternatives.

Going back to the example we used in *Define It*, let's again step into the shoes of my friend at McKinsey & Company, who is figuring out if she wants to stay in consulting.

She really loves consulting, so it's easy for her to imagine staying on track. Yet, in her grandest vision for her career, she also imagines one day starting her own business. Although she has no idea when or how she might do it, she can lay out three tracks in her roadmap.

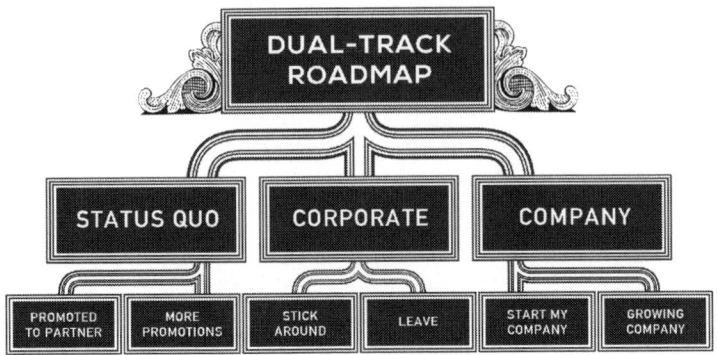

For now, keep it simple. Looking down her status-quo track, she's focused on crushing it at McKinsey & Company and rising to the top. At the same time, she figures that a move to the corporate-side might be a good way to get the experience she wants in starting her own company. And as a third alternative, although it seems a bit too early, she is considering leaving and starting her own company today.

Laying out your roadmap, you clearly see your alternatives, even while you are clearly focused on the track right in front of you. This gives you a way of getting all the thoughts out of your mind and on paper and also gives you a deliberate and thoughtful approach to evaluating your options. From here, it's a matter of determining: *How do I evaluate my options?*

★   ★   ★   ★   ★   ★

CHOICE, THE PROBLEM IS CHOICE

At the end of *The Matrix Reloaded*, having reached what he believed would be his final destination, Neo finally realizes that the path is one of choice. The same is true in navigating your career.

Just laying out your options gets you thinking about how you are driving toward your grandest vision for your career, and it is the choices you make that determine how and whether you get there.

Truth is, evaluating your options and making choices is hard to do, even if you are certain of where you are headed. As you put to work your roadmap, it's still not easy to choose.

While there are many who love their job and will fight retirement, many of us spend our careers unsure. Many in their current jobs spend years dreaming of other roles inside and outside their company.

Yet too many fail to choose.

The biggest risk is not failing to choose whether to stay on track or make a decision to move, it is staying stuck in indecision. Committing neither to your status-quo track or making moves, you risk failing to optimize your career either way.

Celebrated General George Patton once said, "When a decision has to be made, make it. There is no totally right time for anything."

And while I cannot give you guidance on making specific choices that are right for you, I can share something that is typically of greater value: perspectives on making choices in your career.

★ ★ ★ ★ ★ ★

THE POWER OF PERSPECTIVE

In evaluating whether to stay in his career or move to a company, one of my clients presented me with a dozen pages of pros and cons that analyzed the upside and downside.

It was the typical approach you might follow, but after months of thinking, he still found himself stuck and unable to decide.

Without painstakingly working through any of his detailed bullet points (which still had him stuck!), I helped him quickly make a decision by changing the way he was thinking and adding new perspectives. Two ways of adding new perspective are looking forward and backward in your career.

On your roadmap, you begin with the end in mind, framing your choices in the context of your grandest vision for your career. Looking forward and gaining perspective over the long-run can be particularly helpful in making difficult choices, and it can also be helpful to look back on where you have been.

In determining whether to stay on your status-quo track, revisit why you took your job to begin with and also why you are still there. Think back on the steps you have taken and ask yourself:

- *WHY did I join my company?*

- *WHY have I stuck around?*

- *WHAT moves have I considered—taken, and not-taken—and how have my choices crafted my career?*

- *WHAT happens if I do leave? What happens if I don't? What doesn't happen if I do leave? What doesn't happen if I don't?*

I suggest asking a bunch of similar questions, going deep into your past choices, and seeking to understand how you will know you are now making the right choice.

One of my clients said to me, "Looking back, I now see how joining investment banking out of business school was an absolute no-brainer, but the choice to stay is very different."

Another client said that by looking back, he more easily equated his career to the investing axiom: *If you are not selling a stock today, then you are implicitly making the decision to buy.* That idea helped him get focused on why he is choosing to "keep owning" his career.

Conversely, in looking back and seeing that he had stayed in his job five years longer than he planned, my client concluded it was time to leave.

You gain perspective from looking back. And by playing a little scenario analysis, thinking about the choices you have made and how they have played out as well as the options you did not take and where they might have landed you, you are looking at your choices at different levels and adding flexibility to the way you choose tracks in your career.

In adding perspective, you see that while we can often feel like we are at a crossroad, where it is our "one big chance" to do this or that, in hindsight, the options you did or did not take rarely seem that way. By powerfully moving forward, you are always creating more options in your career.

In looking back, you will also likely develop more perspective on your current career. Thinking about how much you have invested gives you a higher appreciation of the importance of first properly considering ways to keep unlocking value in your current career.

In doing this, it is important you are truly, honestly, understanding how much changing your job relates to your career versus you. It's natural to think that the grass is greener in a different job or company, but it rarely is, and a common mistake we make is projecting problems onto your job that really relate to you. As the title of one my favorite books on meditation states: *Wherever You Go, There You Are.*

If you are changing jobs hoping to solve your woes, make sure it isn't you who needs changing!

CHAPTER TWENTY-EIGHT

GETTING IN

Clearly, the decision-making that we rely on in society is fallible. It's highly fallible, and we should know that.

— DANIEL KAHNEMAN

★   ★   ★   ★   ★   ★

Revolutionary personal finance expert Ramit Sethi wrote about a survey that asked people what they would do if they won $10,000. Surprisingly, rather than responding that they would take a vacation or put it toward say, buying a car, the most common response was: *I would save the money to quit my job.*

For years, I dreamed of the day I could quit Goldman Sachs and be free—free of stress, free of voicemail, free of shaving for the man. I figured with my job out of the way, and cash to burn, I would be free to do what I wanted.

But it didn't really end that way.

When I left Goldman to take some time for myself, I discovered that quitting my job didn't miraculously lead me to answers. Instead, I found myself asking a new question: *Now what?*

That experience taught me that while many of us might spend years dreaming of quitting our jobs and landing like Andy Dufresne on the beaches of Zihuatanejo, the truth is this: Our answers do not lie in getting out, but rather on where we want to get in.

A couple of years ago, I read a profile on legendary CEO Bob Pittman, the founder of MTV and former CEO of a number of large companies including AOL, Six Flags, and Century 21 Real Estate.

Having been in what was described as self-imposed corporate exile for a decade, he was quoted as saying, "I've not had my adrenaline pumped up like this in years and I forgot how great it feels… As much as I've denied it by trying to stop working, I am absolutely hard-wired to run companies."

Taking time away from business, he gained perspective. So do not be afraid to mix it up and explore options off the roadmap. There is great advantage in gaining perspectives on your career.

But regardless of whether you stay on your status-quo track or choose any of your alternative tracks, I suggest that rather than focusing on getting out of your current job, remain focused on where you want to get in.

★   ★   ★   ★   ★   ★

THE ROADMAP RULES!

In using your roadmap to choose between your alternative career paths, it's helpful to apply these five principles I call the roadmap rules.

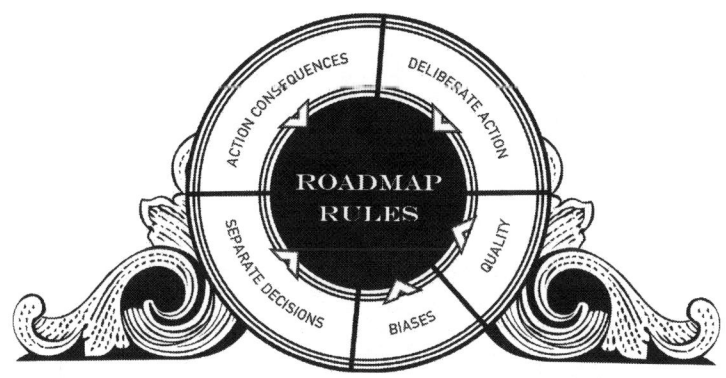

================= RULE 1 =================

DELIBERATE ACTION

The most important benefit of your roadmap is taking a long-term perspective, enabling you to take thoughtful, deliberate action in moving toward your grandest vision for your career. Following Rule 1 means not only deliberately laying out your roadmap but also applying a deliberate approach to making choices.

This means that even if something negative happens, such as failing to get promoted, you never react impulsively. Rather than thinking, *I am underappreciated and it is therefore time for me to leave,* get beyond your initial emotional reaction, go back to your roadmap, and figure out the deliberate actions that will maximize your career. When you remain firmly locked on your grandest vision for your career, you never think about career moves as one-off. Rather, you take deliberate action to keep moving toward what you want.

Taking deliberate action also enables you to think years ahead in building optionality into your career. For instance, if you have spent twenty years in the exact same career, it goes without saying you have significantly limited your flexibility. Looking ahead with a grander vision and taking deliberate action means building optionality into the choices you make throughout your career.

═══ RULE 2 ═══

QUALITY OVER QUANTITY

Rule 2 encourages you to focus on making a small number of high quality moves. While it is true that some people are highly successful at making moves that continually ratchet up their career, more generally, you are better off being incredibly strategic in making moves.

Making moves is risky. You exchange certainty for uncertainty. And you give up a great deal of the value you have accrued in your career.

In leaving one law firm for another, a friend said that what surprised him were the little things he gave up that were hard to replicate. He thought about leaving behind his long-standing relationships, but he missed having someone in a different group who would always be responsive to his call.

As you know, your résumé is delicate, and you want it to convey the right story about you and your career. While I am generally of the view that you can successfully spin any story your audience wants to hear, a cleaner résumé that tells a deliberate story is far easier to sell.

For these and other reasons, I suggest looking at your roadmap like a good judoka, focusing on getting what you want by making the fewest number of high-quality moves.

RULE 3

KNOW YOUR BIASES

What I love about the field of behavioral economics is that in developing awareness of your cognitive biases, you arm yourself for combatting them. The same is true in evaluating options in your career.

Like the concept of sunk costs, you are more likely to think about staying in your current job relative to the investment you have already made. And while that is an important consideration, do not fall into the trap of staying in order to justify your past choices. Instead, get out when it is time for you to leave.

Another obvious bias is the notion that the grass is greener somewhere else. As we have discussed, that is rarely the case, and you best overcome this bias by focusing on getting in and getting perspective.

Another cognitive bias that will keep you in your job is that of avoiding our greatest human fear: uncertainty. As Timothy Ferriss writes in *The 4-Hour Workweek*, "People will choose unhappiness over uncertainty." We are naturally biased to stay where we are rather than moving toward the unknown.

By recognizing these biases, and any others you might have, you bring them to light and give yourself the opportunity to more clearly choose what is right in your career.

SEPARATE DECISIONS

Rather than seeing your decisions as combined, see them as separate.

If you were to sell your old car and buy another, the money you receive from your old car might impact how much you spend on your new car, but you likely see these as two separate and independent decisions. The same is true here.

Your roadmap enables you to carefully and separately evaluate the tracks in your career. Following Rule 4, you simplify your process by asking one question at a time. So rather than asking—*Should I leave my current job to go elsewhere*—you ask two independent questions:

1.   *SHOULD I LEAVE my current job?*

2.   *WHERE should I go?*

In separating the decisions, you are better able to assess the merits of each.

While that might seem impractical because you are evaluating two relative alternatives, it enables you to be intellectually honest about why you are making each decision. Are you taking the other job to escape from your current job, or does the new job stand on its own two feet in helping you get what you want?

Like someone who leaves a bad marriage to jump to another partner, it is not always clear from which perspective you are seeing your choices. By applying Rule 4, you are more likely to make the right choice for the right reasons.

RULE 5

SEPARATE ACTION AND CONSEQUENCE

A common reason people become unable to make career choices is because they are at the same time trying to evaluate the decision to move while also evaluating the consequences.

In evaluating the alternative of staying in your current job or starting your own company, for instance, you might find yourself teetering: *Well, it depends on if I get promoted here and how successful my company will be.*

While that is natural, as long as your decision is tied to the consequences, you are unlikely to ever decide because your answer will be contingent on your absolute certainty and relative optimism for either opportunity, both of which are, of course, unpredictable with absolute certainty!

It is easier to make a decision when you separate your choice from the consequences.

To do this, hold the consequences and focus on your choices. You might ask, for instance: *Not knowing how successful your company will be, are you still willing to give it a shot?* If your answer is "yes," it's easy. If you answer, "no," then you have figured out that your path to making this decision entails developing greater certainty for how successful your company might be.

And if you cannot do that, then by default you are choosing to stay on your current track. Too easy!

CHANGING TRACKS

As I noted earlier, I cannot assess the specifics for evaluating your precise career move. And while assessing the specifics is an important part of evaluating your options, what is often more important is developing a rigorous structure for making good decisions.

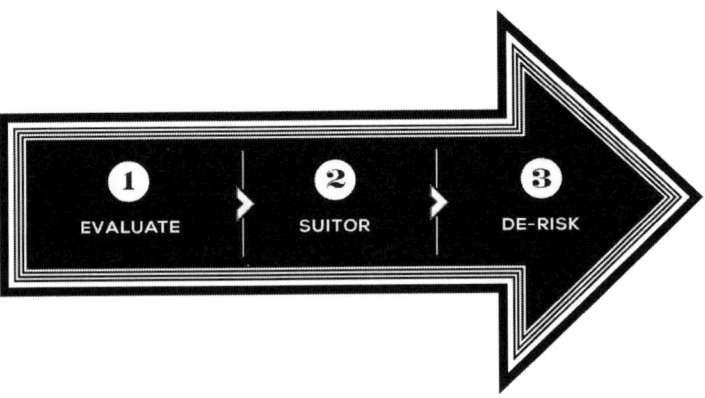

As we move through the three steps of the *Framework of Getting Out*, we will also consider examples of the three types of career moves: moves inside your company, changing companies, and changing careers.

By doing this, we do more than just kill these two topics with the one framework, we also cover these ideas in ascending order related to managing your risk in making moves.

STEP 1

EVALUATING CURRENT POSITION

In Step 1, you carefully analyze your current career track. As we have already touched upon, you should be absolutely certain why you are considering leaving your current job and what you expect to achieve.

Be clear, explicit, and as objective as possible. You want to know with certainty what is lacking in your current career track and how leaving will resolve your problems. In doing this, it is helpful to not only examine your own career but also the careers of your colleagues so that you can clearly identify how much your desire to leave relates to your job versus how your job is working specifically for you. This allows you to identify the core of your grievances and whether they will be resolved in leaving.

Also, at this step, let's consider the least risky of your career moves: making moves inside your company. If this is one of your options, this is by far your lowest risk and perhaps easiest and best way of making moves, so it is worth exploring.

While it's not always easy to affect internal transfers, if you are performing and have strong supporters, your company will likely help you explore changing groups, divisions, or geographies.

═══ S TEP 2 ═══

KNOW THE SUITOR

In Step 1, you carefully evaluate your current track. In Step 2, you go deep into evaluating your alternative track. Doing this, you ensure that each of your decisions stands on its own.

An obvious challenge to knowing the suitor is that as much diligence as you do, you will never be fully able to evaluate another job until you are sitting in your new seat.

That said, you can do plenty of research: 1) First, know the job you are considering; and 2) Know how well you are suited to the job. Both are hard to know. Even the lowest risk move we just covered (making a move inside your company and working in a different group, division, or geography) can be like working in a different industry. You never know until you are there.

So the process is obviously even more complex with the next type of career move—moving to another company in your same profession. Personalities, and differences in culture and roles, can be more extreme than you imagine. If you are staying in the same profession but changing your role you have an even steeper task of not only evaluating your new company, but also evaluating how suited you are to taking on foreign responsibilities.

Candidly, in moving from Goldman Sachs to the Carlyle Group, I got both wrong. My perception was that relative to investment banking investing was more analytically rigorous and stimulating. Also, I got the suitor wrong. From the outside, turning down another job offer from Oaktree Capital and joining Carlyle felt right. But after joining, I thought differently.

In a way, the choice wasn't "wrong" because it allowed me to learn an important lesson so that you won't make the same mistakes. The moral of my story: Use caution with this step. Take your time, and go to the extreme to diligence your suitor, and also how well suited you are to the opportunity.

════ STEP 3 ════

DE-RISK

The third step in the *Framework of Getting Out* is to de-risk your choices. Having carefully evaluated your current career and your alternative, here you're taking other steps to minimize your risk. Here are three ways:

1. THE FIRST WAY to de-risk is following the roadmap rules and doing your best to make good decisions.

   As a reminder, these rules are: Take deliberate action. Consider a small number of high quality moves. Address your biases. Make separate decisions. Separate action and consequence.

   You will be more likely to de-risk your move if you take your time to make deliberate decisions and carefully evaluate your current track and alternatives.

2. ANOTHER WAY TO DE-RISK is to preserve options in your current job. It might feel good to walk into your boss' office and blow off steam on your way out the door, but when you leave quietly you keep good karma around you and potentially preserve options in your career.

3. DO EVERYTHING YOU CAN to check your assumptions and diligence your other alternatives. Don't just carefully evaluate your alternatives, do everything within your power to learn about your options: Seek out references. Talk to those still there and those who have left.

De-risking is important for any move, but it is particularly crucial when it comes to the third type of career move: leaving your current profession and changing careers.

We all have preconceived notions of what it would be like to work in a different career. Many people in professional services have a sense of what it would be like to "go corporate" and many in corporate jobs imagine what it would be like to be at a start-up. And we all imagine what it would be like to work for ourselves.

No matter what the move, however, because you are betting on a company and significantly changing your career, these moves are difficult to de-risk. Only by immersing yourself as much as you can will you have a taste for your fit with the culture and job. As an extreme, you might even consider doing what my client did: Take a couple days off from your current job and go sit at the company, feeling firsthand how it fits.

At the most risky end of the spectrum of getting out is starting something of your own. To an extreme, doing your own thing is the hardest suitor to know and also the most important to de-risk. That said, while this is clearly the highest-risk career move, it's also one you can significantly de-risk. Unlike joining another company, here you have perfect information on defining the opportunity you are creating. And like I did for years, you can take your time to progress your ideas while you are still employed, which gives you plenty of time to keep evaluating this career move.

Doing this not only leads you to make better decisions, but also leads to a higher likelihood of success. As Adam Grant writes in *Originals*, "Entrepreneurs who kept their day jobs had 33 percent lower odds of failure than those who quit."

When considering any big move, try to "add sight." This means to see further down the line. If you are starting your own company, talk to entrepreneurs about what it feels like five or ten years down the road. Doing this you will most certainly gain perspective on your decision.

Having discussed different ways of laying out and evaluating alternative options, let's look at some of the limited thinking that commonly holds people back from getting out and going for what they truly want in their careers.

CHAPTER TWENTY-NINE

WHY YOU WILL NEVER LEAVE!

You're about to jump out a perfectly good airplane, Jonny, how do you feel about that?

— BODHI, *POINT BREAK*

★ ★ ★ ★ ★ ★

It's no secret: Most people will never leave. Most people will never pursue their big goals—forever talking of getting out, but remaining tethered to the same thinking that keeps them chained to their current seat.

Throughout this section, I've given you powerful approaches for evaluating your choices and moving on. But having done this dance a couple of times myself, I know getting out can often require more than powerful frameworks and ways of thinking differently.

If you want to break free, here are the Top 10 limiting thoughts to break.

1

CAUGHT AT THE DOOR

Being caught at the door is exactly what it sounds like—like a parachutist standing at the door: It's his turn. He's got some brawny fellow on his back, and the light is green. He really wants to jump, and he has been building up to this moment for years.

But he cannot. He's stuck there, with one foot in and one foot out the door.

The same can be true in your career. You evaluate whether to stay or leave, and never quite knowing for sure, you do neither. You never fully commit to your current track; you never make a move. You are just stuck there. You might be holding onto your job, but it's unlikely you are getting anywhere.

If you fail to go after your current career track, you run the risk of being pushed out the door. And if you stand up to jump and you whiff, you will lose positioning in your company.

The cold truth is: If you are never going to do it, then stop thinking about leaving and become fully engaged in your career. Too many people live in suffering because they keep dreaming of making career moves they don't have the stomach to make.

Like a man eyeing the beautiful seductress across the room, if you are never going to approach her, save yourself the torment and learn to love the ones you have the courage to land. If you are never going to leave your job, then become excited to stay.

2

STEALING TIME

People fail to make moves because they have too little time to do the work and evaluate their options.

There are two solutions to this problem.

The first is to get serious about how you use your time. If you truly believe that you cannot find a few hours a week to evaluate your career options, then you do not care enough about making a move, or you are resisting doing the work. Both of these are easy to solve with the ideas we have covered in this guide.

A way to make the time is to steal it from your employer. While some walk into the stationary cabinet and steal pens and pads, I suggest stealing your most valuable commodity—time. Just take a look at your schedule, and you will see all the pockets of time you can hijack for your own use.

3

RISK AVERSE

In *Taking Action* we covered the importance of taking risks to get what you want. There, we discussed the ways some people limit their options by identifying themselves as "risk averse."

Nowhere is this idea more limiting than in evaluating your options for getting out. Simply designating yourself as risk averse, you close off your mind to thoughtfully evaluating options.

The truth is: If you are waiting for the risk to be eliminated, you will never move. Making moves is risky, so it requires an appetite for risk and ability to de-risk your moves as much as possible. Making moves can also be costly. In leaving Goldman Sachs I left unvested options and equity on the table, and when I left Carlyle I walked away from two-thirds of my unvested carry income.

But if you're serious about doing what you want, you eat risk and cost.

4

FEEL THE FEAR AND DO IT ANYWAY

In *Feel The Fear And Do It Anyway*, Susan Jeffers writes, "The truth is: If you knew you could handle anything that came your way, what would you possibly have to fear?"

You would likely have fear when getting out, but you wouldn't consider leaving if you did not know you can handle it. So it's just a matter of whether you will do it, irrespective of the fear.

Ask yourself, what are you afraid of?

- FEAR OF FAILURE? How bad can it get? Do you prefer to avoid failure or avoid getting what you want?

- WHAT OTHERS THINK? Which others? Who cares what they think? You're leaving a job they are staying in, so by definition you think differently than them. Why would you care what they think?

- IS IT THE FEAR OF THE UNKNOWN? Good. You should be scared of the unknown. So de-risk it. Add sight. Make it more known.

- IS IT THE STORY YOU ARE RUNNING? Maybe you have a script that sounds something like, *But what if I fail and cannot afford to pay for my children's private school tuition, and we all end up living with my parents, and my kids grow up to be strippers?* Change your stories!

If it's fear, squash it. Then, do it anyway!

5

IT'S NOT ABOUT THE FRIGGIN' IDEA

How many times have you heard some brave fellow from his cushy Aeron seat say, "Man, did you see how she did that? You know, if only I had an idea, I'd be all over that."

Wrong. He wouldn't. Because people who build businesses don't do it because they have an idea; they do it because they are so passionate about creating their own path that they find the idea, or perhaps the idea finds them.

The Everything Store tells the story of where Bezos visits Harvard Business School. After he spoke, the class began dissecting the company's prospects.

Concluding Amazon was toast, they said to Bezos, "You seem like a really nice guy, so don't take this the wrong way, but you really need to sell to Barnes and Noble and get out now."

Getting it wrong is understandable, but the story highlights the difference between the average person attending business school and someone like Bezos who left a top job on Wall Street to start Amazon.

If you are serious about starting something of your own, rather than seeking out the idea, become the sort of person who is bigger than the idea.

The same is true in hunting down another job. Don't wait for that head-hunter to call. Figure out what you want and go after it.

6

MONEY ON YOUR MIND

You are likely earning a decent living in your current job, and it's only natural that you will be thinking about the financial consequences in getting out. It makes sense, but focus on money rationally and accurately.

In considering leaving a well-paying job, many people think they must downgrade their lifestyle, which makes it harder to leave. But this is often false.

In going corporate, one of my clients' salary and bonus were significant compared to his high paying job on Wall Street, and on top of that, he picked up equity and option grants that give him enormous upside far beyond what he could earn in his old job.

Also analyze your "hidden scripts" on money to see which ones lack validity.

For instance, you might have a presupposition that it's bad to take a pay cut, like you are being downgraded in some way. It might be true. You might be downgrading, but what matters is how you choose the meaning.

Why does getting paid less matter? Does it even change your lifestyle? Does it matter to you? What in particular are you giving up?

Be thoughtful about how money feeds into your thoughts about getting out. Money is important, but it deserves far less weight than many people give it.

YOU'RE NOT BANKSY!

Like Banksy, many people are looking to exit through the gift shop, when really, they are more like traveling salesmen, sitting on a plane with the nearest exits either behind or in front of them.

Many spend their career thinking there's some miraculous exit that will one day come their way, when, more accurately, their optionality is generally diminishing over time. While many of us once falsely presumed our options would increase over time, there are really only two effective times to change careers.

The first is when you are junior enough to make a move at the right level. The second is when you are senior enough that you can write your own ticket.

In considering getting out, remain keenly aware of how your options change in your career. Then be incredibly strategic in making moves.

YOLO

You only leave once.

Ugh, I hate that phrase. It's the ultimate default phrase for the risk-averse crowd—the idea that they use to convince themselves they are better off just sticking around than actively managing their career.

It is, of course, mostly true that you only leave once. We all know exceptions, but you may never be able to return to your current job once you leave.

But stop overstating the value!

People with a serious face say, "Yeah, man. It's a silver bullet. You only get one shot to do this right."

What are they talking about? It's a job. It's not like they are defusing a bomb. Surely they have more than one shot.

The other problem with YOLO is that it gets you focused on getting out rather than getting in. Right before one of my girlfriends dumps me, she starts going over the good things she will miss. But if those things were so compelling, she would have never wanted to leave in the first place! The same is true in your career. If your career felt right, you wouldn't want to leave. So stop focusing on what you are losing and focus on where you are headed.

9

IDENTITY

People often tell me that leaving their job is hard because their career is attached to their identity. Now, before I address this idea, let me just say that like most of the field of psychology, this is stupid.

What does it mean to have an identity? Is it who you are right now in your job? With which clients? With which colleagues? Your boss? Your assistant?

I say this idea is stupid because I know your identity is not always the same.

Can you really tell me that you are the same person at work as you are with your mates or at home with your spouse and your kids?

No. It's neither different nor the same because your identity is whatever you choose it to be. If you put on a white t-shirt and started identifying yourself with some group of white t-shirt people, we would laugh at you because it would be meaningless and just as easy for you to whip that white shirt off and put on the black one before changing your identity to another group.

I know that might seem too simple, but like an athlete getting traded to a different team, the name on the back is still the same. It's a job, man. Your identity is not like some business card contest from *American Psycho*. Your identity is who you choose to be.

10

$20 AND DONE

I saved my favorite for last—$20 and done.

I call it that because it's the most common answer to that absurd question you hear throughout your career. You know what I'm talking about, right? That colleague pulls up close to you, puts on his serious voice, and whispers in your ear, "So what's your number?"

That's "$20 and done," because that is sure as hell what you are going to hear from him or her. You're going to hear how with $20 mil in the bank, earning this or that return, you can put away this or that after tax, and that's all you need to live how you want to live.

Sadly, as silly as it sounds, "$20 and done" is a reason seemingly smart people keep grinding it out.

If you want to put away a cool $20 mil after living expenses and taxes, you will be grinding away until you are old and grey and unable to go out and live. And truth be told, you will be there even longer because over time, you will keep pushing up your number. It's a psychological fact that as you make more money, you will spend and want more money. It's called the hedonic treadmill.

Another problem with "$20 and done" is that it creates a deferred-living plan, which suggests that in looking at your life, what you are hoping to have/get/achieve/want is something that is always out in front of you. So, while you are waiting for the day which will never come, this life of yours is passing you by right beneath your growing waistline in your shrinking seat.

Your career is not about getting out but getting in. It's figuring out the career and life you truly want, and then living it. Because then it is never about reaching some bucket of money. You do what you love and get the money flowing from there.

Confucius say, "Choose a job you love, and you will never have to work a day in your life."

CHAPTER THIRTY

BEYOND YOUR CAREER

Nine to five is how you survive, I ain't trying to survive,
I'm tryna live it to the limit and love it a lot.

—JAY-Z, "D'EVILS"

★   ★   ★   ★   ★   ★

You know how they say that no one lies on their death bed wishing they spent another day in the office?

Well, they're wrong.

You see, most of us will never lie on a death bed. One day you will be alive, and the next day you will be dead.

There will be no time of reflection. No one writing a book about your life. You'll be done. Lights out. Game over.

IT'S A JOURNEY, MAN

Transformational thinker Alan Watts once said, "No one imagines that a symphony is supposed to improve as it goes along or that the whole object of playing is to reach the finale. The point of music is discovered in every moment of playing and listening to it."

When the Internet bubble burst and my career outlook quickly and dramatically changed, I stepped back from my career and saw that I was dedicating my life to getting "somewhere." Spending my nights eating dinner at my desk, watching weekends pass by from inside my office, and counting away my years bonus-check to bonus-check, I was deferring my living, sacrificing today for the dream to one day go live my life.

I was giving up today for some idea of how I would be living in the future, even though I had no definition of what this future was or when I would reach it. Also, I could see I ran the risk of becoming stuck on this so-called hedonic treadmill, where this future would never arrive.

Reaching these conclusions I began changing the way I perceived my career and life. Rather than seeing my career as the path to reaching my life, instead I began seeing the two as intertwined.

Whereas in the past, fueled by ideas like "work hard, play hard" and "balancing work and life" I had seen my career and life as separate. I now could see your career is not this "thing" happening separate to your life. It is your life. Your life is the hours you live and breathe, and your career is the largest consumer of most of your hours, most of your life.

In this way, you might see your life as one long highway and just one stretch. Or, as I like to think of it, your career is the v(life: your source of income, how you are driving your life fr(the seat from which you enjoy much of your journey.

As I considered this topic, I began seeing that this notion of separating your work and life is actually a hidden way of saying: *Your work detracts from your life.*

Rubbish! When you love your career, you think different.

DO WHAT YOU WANT!

Famously, Steve Jobs said, "Your work is going to fill a large part of your life, and the only way to be truly satisfied is to do what you believe is great work. And the only way to do great work is to love what you do. If you haven't found it yet, keep looking. Don't settle."

In seeing your career as your vehicle for your life, it is important you keep moving toward what you truly love to do.

Today, too many people are living lives of not-so-quiet desperation. Inside us all, there is a grand vision we have for our careers and lives, yet too few of us are living this vision.

With a lack of definite purpose, too many of us are living well inside our potential, and too few of us stretching our capabilities. We won the genetic lottery. We were born at the right place at the right point in time, with the intelligence and talents to make our careers and lives whatever we want them to be.

Yet, too many of us have settled for some cookie-cutter definition of success. We are slaving away, sacrificing our lives, working hard in our jobs, when it is just as easy to get our jobs working hard for us. Many who enjoy their jobs are considered lucky, when each of us has a vision for the career and life we truly love.

Boldness is bleeding out of us, and we only need to be able to step back and dream, develop the plan to take the steps, and build ourselves into the person who can create the career and life we truly want.

And if you are not going to do that today, when will you do it?

WHAT MORE CAN YOU DO?

Times are tough. Not only is it a hard time for many professionals, but it is especially hard for many others who are far worse off than us.

With many still out of work from the recession and a nascent jobs recovery, and many parts of our economy ravaged by secular change, it's a tough time for many families. And it is a time when those of us blessed with more opportunity have a chance to do more in our world.

More than anything right now, we need more creators. We need more business builders and job creators. We need more smart people doing more things that create value.

We need to get beyond honoring creators like Steve Jobs and instead ask: How do I leave my own dent in the universe?

And while we should certainly admire those like Jeff Bezos for building world-changing companies, we shouldn't stop at admiration. We need more people bold enough to follow their ambitions. Let them inspire us to take action.

WITH THAT, I'LL LEAVE YOU WITH ONE OF
MY FAVORITE QUOTES:

—— 99 ——

Don't ask yourself what the world needs. Ask yourself what makes you come alive and then go do that. Because what the world needs is people who have come alive.

— HOWARD THURMAN

ABOUT THE AUTHOR

A former investment banker and investor, Geoff Blades is an advisor to CEOs and other leaders on corporate and strategic matters as well as topics of personal and professional development.

For Geoff this work began more than fifteen years ago when in his early twenties as an associate in Goldman Sachs' investment banking group, he stepped back from his career and began asking, how do you get what you want in your career and life?

Quickly realizing there was a lack of answers for already highly successful people, Geoff began to research answers for himself.

Putting these ideas to work Geoff transformed his own career on Wall Street, making four job changes at Goldman Sachs, before leaving Wall Street to take eighteen months off to research these topics, before joining the Carlyle Group as a distressed debt investor.

Then, in 2010 Geoff left Wall Street to teach others what had taken him more than a decade to learn.

Today, with more than fifteen years of experience on Wall Street and in researching personal development, and having trained with true masters of personal change, Geoff combines his top-tier business and personal development expertise to deliver a broad range of advisory services to his clients.

Originally from Australia, today Geoff is based in New York.

ACKNOWLEDGMENTS

This guide is the result of the collective efforts of many others: my friends and former colleagues, the authors who have shared their knowledge, my many teachers, and my clients.

I'm deeply indebted to the people of Goldman Sachs who gave me a once-in-a-lifetime opportunity to transform my life. I was a hard-to-please employee, and I'm grateful for the firm's many accommodations.

I owe special thanks to: Jon Aisbitt, David Baxby, Tom Connolly, James Del Favero, Hugo Dudley-Smith, Paul Efron, Andy Gordon, Matthew Koder, Brad Koenig, George Lee, Johan Leven, Rob Pace, Louisa Ritter, Eric Swanson, Gene Sykes, Malcolm Turnbull, and John Waldron.

I am also grateful to my former colleagues at the Carlyle Group. The lessons I learned on the buy-side led me to keep transforming my career. I am particularly thankful to my former team for taking a chance on me, despite my lack of buy-side experience.

I also owe much gratitude to the many clients and management teams I worked with over my years on Wall Street. As an advisor and investor, I had the great privilege of sitting alongside some of the greatest minds in business and investing, learning invaluable lessons each and every day.

My experience on Wall Street formed the foundation, yet it was my thousands of teachers who helped me write this guide.

I, literally, owe my life to the men and women who wrote the books that enabled me to keep taking steps forward.

The many men and women who wrote the books that line my shelves and fill my mind have more than contributed to these ideas: They have contributed to me.

I will never meet many of those who changed my life, some are long gone, but in this guide you see their voices go with me.

I owe more than gratitude to my teachers and trainers. They are the ones who helped me make my most difficult transition and taught me the tools and skills that transformed me and my work.

I'm deeply grateful to Igor Ledochowski, Steve Boyley, Jonny Dupre, Ross Jeffries, John and Kathleen LaValle, John Overdurf, Stever Robbins, Melissa Tiers, and especially to Dr. Richard Bandler, whose shoulders we all stand upon.

I also owe much thanks to the dozens of top teachers I've not yet met, but whose books and video and audio programs have greatly served me, with special thanks to: Tony Robbins, Jack Canfield, Marshall Goldsmith, Michael Hall, Tad James, Eben Pagan, Joe Vitale, and Wyatt Woodsmall.

I am also grateful to Gotham and Deepak Chopra, whose work was particularly instrumental to me when we met some years ago, and who helped me solidify my vision and keep taking steps forward.

I also owe special thanks to Brendon Burchard who taught me not just how far a voice can carry, but also how to keep standing and broadcasting your message. Ditto, with his agent and friend, Scott Hoffman.

I am grateful to my family and friends who have supported me through years of uncertainty and questionable career and life choices! I'm a focused and driven person, and those who journey with me can, at times, carry the burden. It was you who gave me the strength and conviction to keep going.

I'm especially thankful to Mum, who taught me the importance of service and the commitment to never stop doing what you believe in. And to Dad, who is the knower that beyond all this striving, there's simply doing what you want.

I owe much to my private clients—the brave souls who trust me with their minds, careers, and lives. Many of you supported me in my career on Wall Street, and today your trust and commitment has enabled me to keep evolving my work. To you all, I owe more than friendship and my best service.

I owe special thanks to the many reviewers who contributed greatly to these ideas, and to Bid, Adrianna, Erin, Jocelyn, Adam, Al, George, Kat, and Horatio. You have each done for me more than I can say.